From the
Dorothy Jewell
Wettlaufer
Library

1998

THE STILLNESS IN MOVING THINGS

For
Beverly Jarrett

The
Stillness
In Moving Things
The World of Howard Nemerov

William Mills

Memphis State University Press

Manufactured in the United States of America

Library of Congress Cataloging in Publication Data

Mills, William, 1935–
   The stillness in moving things.

   Includes bibliographical references and index.
   1. Nemerov, Howard—Criticism and interpretation.
I. Title.
PS3527.E5Z79   811'.5'4   75-31619
ISBN 0-87870-026-9

The author and publisher are grateful for permission to quote from the following books. The specific references are documented in the footnotes.

   A First Introduction to Existential Phenomenology, by William A. Luijpen and Henry J. Koren. Copyright © 1969 by Duquesne University Press.

   Being and Time, by Martin Heidegger, translated by John Macquarrie. Copyright © 1962 by Harper & Row

   Gnomes and Occasions: Poems, by Howard Nemerov. Copyright © 1973 by Margot Johnson Agency.

   On the Way to Language, by Martin Heidegger, translated by Peter Hertz. Copyright © 1971 by Harper & Row.

   Poetry and Fiction: Essays, by Howard Nemerov. Copyright © 1963 by Rutgers University, the State University of New Jersey. By permission of the Rutgers University Press.

   Recent Philosophy: Hegel to the Present, Etienne Gilson, Thomas Langan, and Armand A. Maurer. Copyright © 1966 by Random House.

   Reflexions on Poetry and Poetics, by Howard Nemerov. Copyright © 1972 by Rutgers University, the State University of New Jersey. By permission of the Rutgers University Press.

   and, of course, to Howard Nemerov for permission to quote from his works.

Contents

Introduction

Howard Nemerov once remarked "for good or ill nobody seems to have much to say *about* what I write. They either dislike it rather harshly, or say it's underrated and very fine . . . but that's about it." Happily, this situation is changing, and one does not need long vision to see that, during the seventies, readings of Nemerov may well appear on the scene with a surge resembling that in Stevens criticism during the fifties and sixties.

When I first undertook this study, there was no extended investigation of Nemerov's poetry in sight. Since that time, however, Julia Bartholomay has published her fine book, *The Shield of Perseus: The Vision and Imagination of Howard Nemerov.*[1] Unaware of her work for some time, I continued my own, completing it with a consideration of the light shed by Nemerov's newest volume, *Gnomes & Occasions.* When I did come upon Ms. Bartholomay's work, I was naturally interested to see whether we had followed the same avenues of investigation. In the main, I concluded, we had not; she has considered the poet's vision through a study of his imagery. Although Ms. Bartholomay and I have pursued different lines of inquiry, and sometimes have reached different conclusions, her analyses of particular poems (especially the "Runes" sequence) are very fine and would be most helpful to any student of Nemerov.[2]

1. Julia Bartholomay, *The Shield of Perseus: The Vision and Imagination of Howard Nemerov* (Gainesville: University of Florida Press, 1972).
2. Within the presentation of my own argument I will refer the reader to Bartholomay's discussions when they seem appropriate.

I have chosen to consider Nemerov's poetry in terms of certain subject matters, in the hope that these divisions might serve to interest new readers (since we are often initially drawn to a person's work for this very reason). And, more importantly, I was engaged by the unique way in which Nemerov approaches these subject matters. There is, of course, the danger of reducing the poems to the particular categories I have chosen, but any point of view has its attendant limitations. Violence will be done to the poems, but it is a real question whether this can ever be avoided in criticism. (And no one has written more eloquently on this question than Joseph Riddel in his study of William Carlos Williams, *The Inverted Bell.*[3]) It is my hope that these "violences" will offer a starting point for reflections.

There will no doubt be profitable studies in the future that will attend to placing Nemerov in relation to his contemporaries and to tradition. I have not undertaken such an investigation; indeed, I think it is likely too early for such work to be fruitful. But, as to twentieth-century movements, Nemerov is clearly a child of his age, specifically an age that includes Wallace Stevens and William Carlos Williams. Nemerov, while dialoguing with "the stillness in moving things," is concurrently dialoguing with his fathers Stevens and Williams, to be sure, and because of his learning, with those of literary tradition in general. He is, too, in that direct line of descent from Donne and the Metaphysicals, with his penchant for metaphors found in the "new science," his wit and love of punning and jokes.

There has been a fair amount of reaction to the poet (though not necessarily to the poems) in the literary quarterlies, and a summary of the reception of his books is readily available in Bowie Duncan's helpful volume *The Critical Reception of Howard Nemerov.*[4] Duncan observes in his introduction that there has been a contradictory critical

3. Joseph N. Riddel, *The Inverted Bell: Modernism and the Counter-poetics of William Carlos Williams* (Baton Rouge: Louisiana State University Press, 1974).
4. Bowie Duncan (ed.), *The Critical Reception of Howard Nemerov: A Selection of Essays and a Bibliography* (Metuchen, N. J.: The Scarecrow Press, Inc., 1971). This book is a valuable reference tool; its bibliography is succinctly

response. Detractors claim the poetry is "academic" and "over-intellectualized," while admirers think of it as "self-reflexive and multifaceted." Both responses are no doubt grounded partially in taste. If one is looking for a response to the world in extravagantly sensuous terms, he will be disappointed with Nemerov's poetry—yet so many of his best poems respond to "deep sayings" found in wild nature. That there might be a mixed response in the romantic sixties could have been expected. Nemerov is not promising apocalypse, or millennium; and he is no darling of the television talk shows.

Julia Bartholomay has observed that "representing no poetic school or movement, Nemerov stands apart in his generation—a giant, if a lonely one, who continues to shun identification with literary fads and bandwagons. Although Louise Bogan cited his work as 'an example of the well-written intelligently ordered poetry that has been termed "academic" by the experimentalists' (and called 'mandarin' by Kenneth Rexroth), Nemerov has not engaged in the cold war between the 'New England Poets' (academicians) and the 'Black Mountain/Beat Group,' representing the short-lived San Francisco Renaissance and the confessional poetry of the fifties and sixties."[5] And for others to describe Nemerov, or any poet, as academic is almost meaningless (unless one decides to use the term as entirely pejorative) when one considers those attached to academies and the spectrum they reveal: from Theodore Roethke, James Dickey, Charles Olson, to Robert Creeley, John Berryman, William Stafford, Richard Wilbur, J. V. Cunningham, and so on.

As I have maintained throughout much of this study, one of Howard Nemerov's importances to us as twentieth-century readers is that his vision has been shaped by a way of seeing, listening, and saying that reflects in turn his own listening to other thinkers' thinking. There are real poets in our time who have been much less aware of certain modern dilemmas and crises, but it is this added dimension of Nemerov's poetry that greatly expands his vision (and which,

---

annotated, and the essays include both overview responses to Nemerov and particular responses to individual volumes.

5. Bartholomay, *Shield of Perseus*, 4–5.

perhaps, excludes some of his audience: how can they respond if they are only vaguely aware of such problems as the
challenges of scientism and some forms of positivism).

Early in Nemerov's work it was clear that he shared with
some of his contemporaries a concern for the problem of
how we know what we know. After his third volume of
poetry, *The Salt Garden,* this concern was omnipresent. As
his way of looking at the world evolved it seems to have
come more and more to resemble that of phenomenologists,
specifically Husserl and his student Heidegger. It is not an
accident that a poet should share some of the same concerns
of these two philosophers. A poet might well feel threatened
and of little value, for example, if the Cartesian view that
mind through *reason* could apprehend objective reality was
unassailable. Hume hardly helped matters by saying that the
mind knew nothing at all. Kant, of course, met the problem,
and to some extent, Husserl and Heidegger moved from his
work to positions that are crucially different. Initially I
turned to Husserl and his interpreters to confirm this approach to Nemerov, and after reading Riddel's *Inverted Bell,*
my attention was directed to certain works of Heidegger
(particularly *On the Way to Language*[6]). What struck me were
the similarities in Nemerov's and Heidegger's vision, and
sometimes language. Such similarities will hopefully be apparent enough that the recognition will prompt further investigation by others.

The importance of phenomenology and Heidegger for
poets is that such a thing as lyric poetry would not be
shunned as some kind of mere expressive meaning, or pseudo-
statement, but would in fact be regarded as authentic statement. Scientific knowledge is not considered the only kind of
statement with real value. The poet becomes very important,
especially for a time which Heidegger would call the "mid-
night of the world." Poetry is respectful of things in a way
that scientism is not. Thus, in a very important way,
Nemerov speaks to us and reminds us, as he writes in "The
Blue Swallows," that "Finding again the world, / That is the
point, where loveliness / Adorns intelligible things. . . ."

6. Martin Heidegger, *On the Way to Language,* trans. Peter D. Hertz (New
York: Harper & Row, 1971).

I have not included any biographical summary, for both Duncan and Bartholomay have such summaries. Presently Nemerov is teaching at Washington University in St. Louis. One of the most important biographical events, as far as Nemerov's audience is concerned, was his move in 1948 to Vermont, where he taught at Bennington College until 1966. From this landscape have come many of his finest poems. It seems to have been here that Nemerov began to "listen" so attentively to nature, "to find again the world." What I would like to argue is that "listening" for Nemerov (what he calls his "aural imagination") is clearly similar to the "listening" Heidegger urges. Nemerov does not mean, I contend, "aural" in the sense of hearing the sound of a car or a bird; if he did one might expect a preponderance of honking and chirping in the poems. Rather, he means an imagination that has opened itself up to being, has stopped and listened to being. In this way the imagination is the agent of reality. The rhythm that he speaks of hearing is the rhythm of being.

There is another side to the poetry, one that appears when the poet senses and/or becomes enraged at inauthentic behavior or "idle" talk. This might be a minister seeing a boom in religion as a result of increased affluence, as related in the poem "Boom!"—or groundless talk, hearsay, and gossip becoming the false basis for foolish, and destructive, action. I have discussed the poetry that engages such inauthentic activity in the chapter entitled "The Urban Landscape." Though there are those readers who see Nemerov's work as deeply divided, the poet himself feels that at bottom there is a unity. And it may be that such a unity exists as two sides of a coin: language mirroring authentic experience; or language mirroring nothing at all, and as such meaningless.

It is perhaps to be expected that a poet who writes such a self-reflexive poetry would write about poetry itself, that he would be intensely concerned with language and metaphor. The problem involving language's relation to person (or poet) and thing is being vigorously pursued today and has been vigorously pursued in the past. Nemerov participates in this saying about Saying, and as I have attempted to show, sometimes takes over the language of language philosophy and, in particular, Heideggerian analysis. He echoes Heidegger's observation that "Poetry and thinking are modes of saying. The nearness that brings poetry and thinking together into neighborhood we call Saying. Here, we assume, is the essential nature of language. 'To say,' related to the Old Norse 'sage,' means to show: to make appear, set free, that is, to offer and extend what we call World, lighting and concealing it. This lighting and hiding proffer of the world is the essential being of Saying."[7]

If Heidegger is correct in his notion that poetry is in touch with the ground of being, that language, and especially the language of poetry, gives authentic being to things, and if it is also true that Nemerov is responding in such a way to being, to "the stillness in moving things," then perhaps Nemerov may be considered much more than the "poet of minimal affirmation" he has been labeled.[8]

7. *Ibid.,* 93.
8. Duncan (ed.), *The Critical Reception of Howard Nemerov,* 29.

Poetry
IL   *The Image and the Law.* New York: Henry Holt, 1947.
GR   *Guide to the Ruins.* New York: Random House, 1950.
SG   *The Salt Garden.* Boston: Little, Brown and Co., 1955.
MW *Mirrors & Windows: Poems.* Chicago: University of Chicago Press, 1958.
NSP *New & Selected Poems.* Chicago: University of Chicago Press, 1960.
NRD *The Next Room of the Dream.* Chicago: University of Chicago Press, 1962.
BS   *The Blue Swallows.* Chicago: University of Chicago Press, 1967.
G&O *Gnomes & Occasions: Poems.* Chicago: University of Chicago Press, 1973.

Prose
PF   *Poetry and Fiction: Essays.* New Brunswick, N.J.: Rutgers University Press, 1963.
RPP *Reflexions on Poetry & Poetics.* New Brunswick, N.J.: Rutgers University Press, 1972.

THE STILLNESS IN MOVING THINGS

"Because the mind's eye lit the sun"

One element in the poetry of Howard Nemerov that urges his relevance to contemporary audiences is his awareness of the main currents of thought during his own time. He does not write as if he lived in a pre-Cartesian world or as if the Einsteinian world picture had not come along. As poet and thinker he has taken the problems of his day seriously, engaged them, and this engagement is an intrinsic part of his value.

Nowhere is this awareness of the ideas of the times more apparent in Nemerov's work than in the area of epistemology. By "awareness" I do not mean that Nemerov has any systematic epistemological position. He may have, but his poetry would not be the likely place to present it. What one does find is an intelligence that is perfectly content to doubt itself in much the way that philosophy has had to do. There is a sufficient number of poems in the collected poetry to indicate that epistemology is a major concern and, in addition, a concern that has been a source of considerable interest and even anxiety for him.

"Solipsism & Solecism" (*G&O*) dramatize this particular species of anxiety in a particularly witty way.

Strange about shadows, but the sun
Has never seen a single one.
Should night be mentioned by the moon
He'd be appalled at what he's done.

"Turning on the light" of human perception may create as many problems as it solves. The poem emphasizes, too, the prison of the point of view. As soon as one moves about an object, he ceases to see the other side. The prison of solipsism quite naturally leads to anxiety and despair. The very etymology of solipsism associates itself with the modern preoccupation with "aloneness." Punning on *solecism*, the sun has not seen "a single one," the solecism itself. The sun would be "appalled," or would "pale," if he knew.

Nemerov's well-known poem "The Blue Swallows" is an example of poetry about the mind thinking. The speaker in the poem is on a bridge looking across a millstream and below him he sees seven blue swallows flying. Invisible paths of flight stick for a moment in the mind, then dissolve. The speaker considers how often the mind creates relationships that are no more the "fact" than the non-existent "designs" that have been created by the seven blue swallows.

> Thus helplessly the mind in its brain
> Weaves up relation's spindrift web,
> Seeing the swallows' tails as nibs
> Dipped in invisible ink, writing . . .

The speaker then goes on to enumerate some of the various kinds of "spindrift web" that man has woven.

> Poor mind, what would you have them write?
> Some cabalistic history
> Whose authorship you might ascribe
> To God? to Nature? Ah, poor ghost
> You've capitalized your Self enough.

So much then for theology, and for Nature as God's "handiwork." He goes on to remind us that William of Occam "took care of" this problem a long time ago. This habit of the mind, of "weaving up relation's spindrift web," or of conjuring general concepts or universals, has no substance, in one sense of the word, and thinking that it does leads one astray:

> That villainous William of Occam
> Cut out the feet from under that dream
> Some seven centuries ago.
> It's taken that long for the mind
> To waken, yawn and stretch, to see
> With opened eyes emptied of speech
> The real world where the spelling mind
> Imposes with its grammar book
> Unreal relations on the blue
> Swallows.

Here the speaker might with Bertrand Russell say, "Gradually Occam's razor gave me a more clean-shaven picture of reality." What follows in the poem is very suggestive of the poet's idea of the relationship the mind might have with that which is outside itself and, further, is an example of the affirmation the poet can make.

> Perhaps when you will have
> Fully awakened, I shall show you
> A new thing: even the water
> Flowing away beneath those birds
> Will fail to reflect their flying forms,
> And the eyes that see become as stones
> Whence never tears shall fall again.
>
> O swallows, swallows, poems are not
> The point. Finding again the world,
> That is the point, where loveliness
> Adorns intelligible things
> Because the mind's eye lit the sun.

Just as we have learned that our general concepts and myths are constructs of our own doing and bear no relation *neces-*

sarily to the "world of things," likewise we may learn to "see," with increasing precision, "things as they are." I think Nemerov would care to stress in such a statement the word "increasing." This is to say, a dynamic process that perhaps by necessity does not reach an end. Our experience would lead us to form this conclusion. Gradually we may learn to see better through the efforts of the poet, the scientist, and the philosopher.[1]

Elsewhere Nemerov has written on similar matters, and it is to the point to introduce his remarks here. His essay, "The Poetry of Wallace Stevens," is very helpful in illuminating that poet's attitude toward the relation between mind and reality and is, incidentally, useful in describing Nemerov's own poetry. While he is suggesting an explanation for Stevens' choice of metaphor and its seemingly arbitrary character, he says that he ran upon a description of "the school of existential thought known as phenomenology" in Albert Camus' *The Myth of Sisyphus,* and it struck him as relevant to Stevens' way of approaching reality, or at least to his theory that the choice of metaphor for describing reality is arbitrary. There may be a common ground in Nemerov's own poetry. The passage from Camus concerns Edmund Husserl, the founder of phenomenology:

> Originally Husserl's method negates the classic procedure of the reason. . . . Thinking is not unifying or making the appearance familiar under the guise of a great principle. Thinking is learning all over again how to see, directing one's consciousness, making of every image a privileged place. In other words, phenomenology declines to explain the world, it wants to be merely a description of actual experience. It confirms absurd thought in its initial

---

1. A variant reading of lines 29–35 might be, of course, that in death these false conjurings or errors do not continue; thus tears do not fall where, assuredly, they do not. Such a vision might come only with the loss of what makes us human.

assertion that there is no truth, but merely truths. . . . Consciousness does not form the object of its understanding, it merely focuses, it is the act of attention, and, to borrow a Bergsonian image, it resembles the projector that suddenly focuses on an image. The difference is that there is no scenario, but a successive and incoherent illustration.[2]

To begin with, the idea that "thinking is not unifying or making the appearance familiar under the guise of a great principle," that it is "learning all over again how to see, directing one's consciousness, making of every image a privileged place," is very similar to the theme of "The Blue Swallows." Further, this posture has been a fairly consistent one with Nemerov.

"To find again the world" is used here in a special sense. How exactly is this "finding" different from other ways already known? Nemerov has, in the first place, ruled out understanding particulars in terms of "a great principle," or some "cabalistic history." But what about finding the world by simply looking at "actual experience" in the way that scientists are doing every day? Surely physical science pretends to study experience without imposing "relation's spindrift web." How is this to be understood as any different from the phenomenologist's contention that he is "really" doing it?

I have turned to a contemporary exponent of phenomenology, William Luijpen, for some definitions and distinctions that help to clarify the questions, for a description of the phenomenologist's position concerning scientism, and in turn the alternative way of looking at things advanced by Husserl. I have done this instead of looking at Husserl's basic writings in the interest of clarity and brevity.[3] On the matter

2. Nemerov quotes Camus in *Poetry and Fiction: Essays* (New Brunswick: Rutgers University Press, 1963), 79–80.
3. For an introduction to Husserl, see his *Phenomenology and the Crisis of Philosophy,* trans. with an introduction by Quentin Lauer (New York: Harper & Row, 1965). For a deeper investigation *Cartesian Meditations,* tr. Dorion Cairns

of scientific knowledge Luijpen writes that scientists think *their* science at least gives us "genuine and reliable knowledge."

> Such an attitude, however, contains a philosophy which is in principle "complete." One who simply identifies physical science with genuine and reliable knowledge decrees that knowledge, *tout court,* is the kind of knowledge offered by physical science. But it is obviously beyond the competency of physical science to define what knowledge, *tout court,* is; that is the task of the philosopher. Moreover, one who proposes a "complete" theory of knowledge cannot avoid proposing also a "complete" theory of reality. For, no matter how he wishes to define knowledge, he cannot escape from admitting that knowledge, unlike dreaming, is a disclosure of reality. Thus, by absolutizing physical science, he proposes as a "complete" theory of reality that whatever cannot be disclosed by science is simply not real. Again, however, it is not the task of the physicist to define what reality, *tout court,* is; that task belongs to the philosopher.

> *Scientism* is the name given to the absolutism of science, understood in the narrow sense of physical science, for until recently all positive sciences were defined as "still imperfect forms of physical science." But scientism is an internal contradiction. By claiming that meaningful statements are statements of physical science, it implies that other kinds of state-

(The Hague: Nijhoff, 1960), and *Ideas,* tr. W. R. Boyce-Gibson (New York: Macmillan, 1941). Quentin Lauer has also written a fine commentary on Husserl and phenomenology entitled *Phenomenology: Its Genesis and Prospect* (Harper & Row, New York, 1965).

ments are nonsense. Now, this claim itself obviously is not a statement of physical science and therefore must be classified as a nonsense statement. Those who make the claim, however, imply that it is a meaningful statement; hence the contradiction.[4]

Of course such a distinction between "scientific" knowledge and "another" kind of knowledge about particular things does not yet explain how Nemerov means "Finding again the world / . . . where loveliness / Adorns intelligible things," but it is a necessary starting point.

Existential phenomenologists claim that they have overcome the divorce, apparent since Descartes, between the knowing subject and the world outside him. Luijpen notes, "Since Descartes philosophers accepted without question that knowledge was a mirroring of brute reality and that physical science was *the* system of objective mirror images."[5] Once the divorce between subject and world was introduced, there was the choice of emphasizing consciousness or the world—idealism or realism. This divorce does not exist, claims the phenomenologist. A brief summary of the phenomenological position as related by Luijpen may prove useful here.

If one wishes to speak about a blooming tree in a meadow, physical science can say something about the tree and the perception of it, *e.g.,* physical and physiological processes. "But what sense does it make to wish to speak *only in this way* about the perception of a blooming tree in the meadow."[6] The blooming tree can be fragmented, or "atomized," but this information is not more "objective," when it comes to perceiving a tree. The tree is not a series of processes for us, but a blooming tree in a meadow and physics or some other science is not competent to explain it to us as it is. It is not that what a science may say about the cerebral processes is untrue, but when scientists speak of such

    4. William A. Luijpen and Henry J. Koren, *A First Introduction to Existential Phenomenology* (Pittsburgh: Duquesne University Press, 1969), 9–10.
    5. *Ibid.,* 55–56.
    6. *Ibid.,* 59.

things, *"they do not speak of anything at all"* unless ultimately they are trying to speak of the perception of the
blooming tree in the meadow."[7] When Husserl says ''Back to
the things themselves" he means for us to go back to such an
"original" experience—an integral way of knowing something
as it occurs.

> Knowledge is not a matter of "strong cog-
> nitive images" in the subject's interiority, but
> the *immediate* presence of the subject as a
> kind of "light" to a present reality. Knowl-
> edge is a mode of man's being-involved-in-the-
> world. The subject, then, is not "first" and in
> himself a kind of "psychical thing" which
> "subsequently" enters into relationship with
> physical things through cognitive images.
> Knowledge is not a relationship between two
> different realities, but is the subject himself
> involved in the world.[8]

Whatever violence has been done by summarizing Luijpen's
analysis of this position, I think the general outlines remain
intact.

The closing lines of "The Blue Swallows," "Finding
again the world / . . . where loveliness / Adorns intelligible
things / *Because* the mind's eye lit the sun" (italics mine)
may help to suggest Nemerov's general concept of *how* man
knows. It may even be necessary to *find* the world again
because science has atomized experience. Luijpen's example
of a blooming tree in a meadow demonstrates that physical
science does not speak about a "blooming tree in a meadow";
likewise physical science does not speak about "loveliness."
It must be said that Nemerov does not single out physical
science in his poem, but physical science is included by
implication.

7. *Ibid.,* 60.
8. *Ibid.,* 61.

And how does the mind's eye light the sun? From the phenomenologist's position, knowledge is the *immediate* presence of the subject as a kind of "light" to a present reality. Perhaps this is the way the world can be "found" again, a world where "loveliness" is still a meaningful reality. This is so only because the mind's eye lights the sun.

In a similar vein I think the poem "Celestial Globe" (*BS*) reflects this human knowledge as "intentionality" (as the phenomenologist likes to name this *"immediate* presence of the subject as a kind of 'light' to a present reality"). In a characteristic Hamlet-like stance of meditating on skull-surrogates of some kind, the Nemerovian speaker holds a celestial globe in his hand and pursues the associations. At one point in the action the speaker takes the hollow sphere and wears it on his head:

> As a candle wears a pumpkin
> At Halloween, when children
> Rise as the dead; only
> It has no human features,
> No access to its depths
> Whatever, where it keeps
> In the utter dark
> The candle of the sun,
> The candle of the mind,
> Twin fires that together
> Turn all things inside out.

One of the *données* of the Nemerovian world is of course a universe that "keeps / In the utter dark" the inquiring mind. The speaker in the poem, like Nemerov himself, never has to worry, though, about running out of a sense of mystery, a fear many may have had from various demythologizing efforts of man. It is a world that does not seem to have any "access to its depths / Whatever." Yet somehow the poem does not seem to end on a note of complete negation. There remain the powers of the "candles" of the sun and the mind. These powers have the ability to "turn all things inside out."

There are many rich possibilities to this last line. The sun was described as a "great source" which "Is blazing forth his fires." In a very literal way the sun's insides, the source, are turned from inward, outward. The sun, too, is the power that turns the inward seed outward to life. In the second section of the poem, the mind is "turning things inside out." Homer is the "dark fire fountaining forth / The twin poems of the war / And of the journey home—."

It is apparent that this poem was not written with a "diagram" of phenomenology by which the poet simply fleshed out the model with concrete examples for the reader's quicker retention. If there is a departure from the basic attitude, though, it is a drift inward, a drift that sometimes appears to return to psychologism. This seems to be the limit of the movement.

Another *Blue Swallows* poem, "The Rope's End," also touches on the kind of knowledge that physical science arrives at because of its methods.

> Unraveling a rope
> You begin at an end.
> Taking the finished work
> You pick it to its bits,
>
> Straightening out the crossed,
> Deriving many from one,
> Moving forward in time
> And backward in idea . . .
>
> . . . .
>
> Having attained the first
> Condition, being dust,
> No longer resembling rope
> Or cord or thread or hair,
>
> And following no line:
> Incapable of knot or wave
> Or tying things together
> Or making anything secure,

Unable to bind, or whip
Or hang till dead. All this
In the last analysis
Is crazy man's work,

Admitted, who can leave
Nothing continuous
Since Adam's fall
Unraveled all.

The idea is clear enough. The basic sentiment has a romantic emphasis about it. The image works very effectively in describing a functional object that has meaning as long as it is whole (tying things together and making them secure), an object that becomes useless after its atomization (unable to serve as whip or hangman's noose).

Nemerov obviously understands that a scientist (or engineer) needs to take things apart in order to understand them or make them better. But the poem is about taking things apart, like "a blooming tree in a meadow," things which do not have the same reality once they are disintegrated. The "last analysis" of line 27 is the very last analysis and is indeed "crazy man's work."

The same theme can be found, if somewhat more internalized, in "Endegeeste," a poem from *Mirrors and Windows,* which Nemerov published nine years earlier. The scene in this poem is a view of Endegeeste, formerly a residence of Descartes and now a state insane asylum. Reading, and reflecting on the scene outside the window, the speaker sees a resemblance between his own situation and that of Descartes':

I live in a great and terrifying time,
As Descartes did. For both of us the dream
Has turned like milk, and the straight,
        slender tree
: Twisted at root and branch hysterically.

I keep my reasonable doubt as gay
As any—though on the lawn they seem to say

Those patient, nodding heads, "sum, ergo sum."
The elms' long shadows fall cold in my room.

The notion of a disorientation or a disintegration of the
psyche or mind is associated with disintegration of the
subject-object relation in a fashion somewhat like the one in
"The Rope's End." Nemerov even speculates that the world
exhibits enough absurdity and madness to have been created
with a circular causality. The "steady state" cosmology of
the chicken-and-the-egg puzzle is suggested in "Creation
Myth on a Moebius Band" from his latest volume, *Gnomes &
Occasions:*

This world's just mad enough to have been made
By the Being his beings into Being prayed.

"Idea" (*NRD*) reflects the tension with which the poet
considers the mind's abstract capabilities. The tension seems
to result from an admiration of abstraction and a sense of its
destructiveness:

Idea blazes in darkness, a lonely star.
The witching hour is not twelve, but one.
Pure thought, in principle, some say, is near
Madness, but the independent mind thinks on
Breathing and burning, abstract as the air.

Supposing all this were a game of chess.
One learned to do without the pieces first,
And then the board; and finally, I guess,
Without the game. The lightship gone adrift,
Endangering others with its own distress.

O holy light! All other stars are gone,
The shapeless constellations sag and fall
Till navigation fails, though ships go on

> This merry, mad adventure as before
> Their single-minded masters meant to drown.

In the first stanza there is again the association of madness with unbalanced modes of knowledge as in "Endegeeste" and "The Rope's End." In the second stanza one line of consequence is compared to a chess game, whose rules and values are arbitrary to begin with. Finally these are "abstracted" out of existence, even the game itself. The "lightship" of idea which "blazes in darkness" goes adrift, endangering others. The third stanza examines another line of consequence of abstraction. With idea as "polestar," and that only, the light of the other stars is not apparent. The old constellations in the form of mythological figures derived from imaginary lines are no longer to the point; modern astronomy considers them abstractly. Abstraction of the heavens is rendered through the symbolic language of mathematics. With only the "polestar" of idea to guide the navigators, these "single-minded masters" are meant to drown.

The poem "Thought" (*BS*) is about the mind as it turns to itself. It begins, "thought is seldom itself / And never itself alone. It is the mind turning / To images." This says that thought is only thought when it is thinking *about* something. (This is precisely the assertion of phenomenological "Intentionality.") Much of the time this "something" takes the form of images. The second section of this poem offers a little drama of process and reveals an attitude about the mind's conclusion concerning reality.

> Leaves shaken in the wind
> Rattle the light till shadows
> Elide, and yet the grass
> Bends to the weight of the wind
> And not the shadows' weight.
> The minnow-waves can mingle
> In shallows at the shore
> As if they were no matter,
> Until they peak and break,

Taking the sunlight up
In a shatter of spray.

Matter is therefore real. The last section, however, proves somewhat difficult.

And mind in some such way
Passing across the world
May make its differences
At last unselfishly
The casualties of cause:
    Its likeness changes.

The mind may make the differences, the "apparent" differences and discrepancies, the "casualties" of the process of cause and effect. After this, the mental event, "The likeness changes," the image of the world *for now* is focused in the way Camus describes it in *The Myth of Sisyphus.*

No matter how often Nemerov may disparage a useless fragmentation of the analytical process, he is emphatic about not preferring "cabalistic histories" or an unjustified explanation of particular experience in terms of some General Principle. "The Loon's Cry" (*MW*) is a case in point. As the speaker takes a walk in the cold evening, he is intensely aware of the natural world around him. But he is not permitted to be "Nature's priest" in the way Wordsworth or someone like him would be. As the setting sun's ball of fire is imaged in the sea, the moon is somehow balanced in the river on the other side of him. The balance is striking. However there is a significant difference in this poet's response to the moment.

But I could think only, Red sun, white moon,
This is a natural beauty, it is not
Theology. For I had fallen from
The symboled world, where I in earlier days
Found mysteries of meaning, form, and fate
Signed on the sky, and now stood but between
A swamp of fire and a reflecting rock.

What is left of interest when the "symboled world" has fallen? As the speaker continues to reflect (midway in the walk) he concludes that "We'd traded all those mysteries in for things, / For essences in things, not understood—." But as the poet "listens to nature speak," even this possibility is not permitted.

> As answering my thought a loon cried out
> Laughter of desolation on the river,
> A savage cry, now that the moon went up
> And the sun down—yet when I heard him cry
> Again, his voice seemed emptied of that sense
> Or any other, and Adam I became,
> Hearing the first loon cry in paradise.

Not even the substantiality of a reality in things is allowed. The man thinks *now* he understands what that cry meant. The loon's laughter does not seem to ridicule the idea that there is a fundamental force behind a constantly changing reality, although it does seem to deride any notion of a static idea or a static reality. The poet is driven to celebrate this force. As he celebrates it, he considers the moon, which may have been a living and changing world like the one he lives on, and then he considers the stars:

> Chaos of beauty, void,
> O burning cold, against which we define
> Both wretchedness and love. For signatures
> In all things are, which leave us not alone
> Even in the thought of death, and may by arts
> Contemplative be found and named again.

These signatures are not derived from any immanence that rests in fixed things, no "symboled world," but truths of a changing reality that are what they are because of their relationship with man, the poet. Finding and naming these signatures in things is like the theme in "The Blue Swallows" of "Finding again the world . . . where loveliness / Adorns intelligible things." It is interesting to note Stephen Daedalus' thoughts about "signatures" in the beginning of the third chapter of *Ulysses.*

> Ineluctable modality of the visible: at least that if no more, thought through eyes. Signatures of all things I am here to read, seaspawn and seawrack, the nearing tide, that rusty boot. Snotgreen, bluesilver, rust: coloured signs.

Joyce's conception of "signatures" may not be the same as Nemerov's, but the resemblance is striking.

At this point in "The Loon's Cry" the speaker thinks he may hear the bird mocking this notion that truths may be found in the changing reality.

> The loon again? Or else a whistling train,
> Whose far thunders began to shake the bridge.
> And it came on, a loud bulk under smoke,
> Changing the signals on the bridge, the bright
> Rubies and emeralds, rubies and emeralds
> Signing the cold night as I turned for home,
> Hearing the train cry once more, like a loon.

How is the tension of ideas resolved in this last stanza? Or is it even resolved? The train shakes the very bridge that the speaker views and which acts as the dividing fulcrum of the initial experience of balance: red sun, white moon. The bridge is not only not static and certain, but the train changes the signals on the bridge. As Nemerov presents the signals, the effect is not to suggest a change from red to green, but rather changing, alternating stop and go, "signing the cold night." And now that the signatures have been "found and named again," what is the relation to man? Perhaps the signature is not ambivalent, but *about* ambivalence, and about the ambiguity and mystery that constitute the world. The last "cry" of the train, "like a loon," is only a *double entendre* to an already haunting ambiguity.

"The Sanctuary," in the 1950 volume *The Salt Garden,* is an early analog of the mind and its habits. This is, incidentally, the first volume to reflect the writer's move from the city to the countryside of Vermont. It seems that as he "listens" to Nature, he discovers appropriate correlatives for his mental events with much more frequency. In "The Sanctuary" trout suspended in the water of a clear mountain stream suggest thinking.

> . . .like thoughts emerging
> Into a clear place in the mind, then going back,
> Exchanging shape for shade.

At such moments his past and his own body seem to dissolve; as he becomes mind, all motion and change seem to stop.

> Even at such times
> The mind goes on transposing and revising
> The elements of its long allegory
> In which the anagoge is always death;
> And while this vision blurs with empty tears,
> I visit, in the cold pool of the skull,
> A sanctuary where the slender trout
> Feed on my drowned eyes . . . Until this trout
> Pokes through the fabric of the surface to
> Snap up a fly. As if a man's own eyes
> Raised welts upon the mirror whence they stared,
> I find this world again in focus, and
> This fish, a shadow dammed in artifice,
> Swims to the furthest shadows out of sight
> Though not, in time's ruining stream, out of mind.

The mind that participates in this "transcendental" experience does not fall away in thoughtlessness, but continues as if by reflex to consider itself. The trout seem to feed on his eyes. The speaker has achieved some kind of terrifying oneness with the world outside his mind, until, literally, the trout breaks through the water to catch a fly and fractures the smooth film of the surface of the water. Figuratively the world outside his mind, the quiddity of things, seems to invade his mind violently. Or, the *persona* reflects, did his mind raise "the welts upon the mirror"; did he create what reality there was to this moment? Then the "picture" or image is once again in "focus." The perspective is righted. But the speaker does not forget what an awesome and mysterious sequence took place during this time when the mirror was distorted. In this surreal drama, this fish, "like thought," swims back to the subterranean places in the mind, out of sight of consciousness; but the mind knows it was there and it is not out of mind. A poem like "The Sanctuary" is a good example of the modern sensibility in action. Nature poetry can never be quite the same because of this sensibility.

"This, That & the Other" (*BS*) is a dialogue between two attitudes concerning knowledge and reality, those of physics and theology. The subtitle is much to the point: "a dialogue in disregard." The scene of the poem (or dialogue) is a pond. Two figures (THIS and THAT) watch the snowflakes fall on the water and as they watch them they comment on the meaning of the phenomenon. THIS apparently is speaking from the point of view of the physicist, although he could be any realist. Like the symboled world of "The Loon's Cry," this world has fallen, or else never existed for this character. He comments in a commonsensical fashion. His quasi-courteous companion considers the same phenomenon, but "interprets" it in terms of hermetic doctrine.

>   THIS: Though I get cold, and though it tells me
>   nothing
>   Or maybe just because it tells me nothing,
>   I have to stand and watch the infinite white
>   Particulate chaos of the falling snow.
>   . . . .

THAT: The things below are as the things above.
A parable of universal love,
To see the water taking in the snow.

THIS says that his companion can thus interpret if he cares to, but in fact he thinks, "There's no more reason in it than in dreams." The answer does not deter THAT for a moment:

THAT: Then I'll interpret you this dream of yours
And make some sense of it; rather, of course,
Some mind of it, for sense is what you make,
And your provision is for me to take.
First, I observe a pretty polarity
Of black and white, and I ask, could this be
A legend of the mingling of the races?

THAT continues as hermetic theologian throughout the little drama. THIS observes in the middle of the dialogue that "One of the things [the surface of the water] does / Is mirror, and there's a model for all thought." This seems to describe the view of the "naive realist" that Luijpen attacked. Luijpen maintained that one really could not speak about the problem of knowledge from this position, but must become philosophical, something which THIS is avoiding. THAT "philosophizes" but THIS murmurs "sleeveless speculation" to such thinking.

What is ironic is the last speech of the dialogue which is uttered by "Both."

The Other is deeply meddled in this world.
We see no more than that the fallen light
Is wrinkled in and with the wrinkling wave.

It seems clear that the naive realist and the hermetic theologian can make the same statement about "The Other" and not mean the same thing, and in fact "disregard" each other's approach to reality altogether. This is possible because "The Other is deeply meddled in this world."

The difficulty or even impossibility of grasping the whole of life Nemerov dramatizes in "Angel and Stone" (*NSP*). One of the habitual scenes for the reflecting "I" in Nemerov's brooding lyrics appears in this poem: a pool of water whose surface serves as a mirror of reality. In this instance, the figure who looks into the pool thinks that so much of the difficulty of understanding the nature of things results from the perceiver's inevitably self-centered position.

> In the world are millions and millions of men,
>   and each man,
> With a few exceptions, believes himself to be
>   at the center,
> A small number of his more or less necessary
>   planets careering
> Around him in an orderly manner, some
>   morning stars singing together,
> More distant galaxies shining like dust in any
>   stray sunbeam
> Of his attention. Since this is true not of one
>   man or of two,
> But of ever so many, it is hard to imagine
>   what life must be like.

One might derive an orderly system of some sort that could account for the whole of things and the order of such a system appears beautiful. The poet uses the example of a stone cast into the middle of a pool. The concentric circles that move out from it and that touch the limits of the pool only to return to the center of the order-creating stone are beautiful. This same situation obtains if two stones are cast, because the angularities of the intersecting lines are interesting and beautiful: this phenomenon is not yet too complex to be understood and rewarding.

But if you throw a handful of sand into the
water, it is confusion,
Not because the same laws have ceased to
obtain, but only because
The limits of your vision in time and number
forbid you to discriminate
Such fine, quick, myriad events as the angels
and archangels, thrones
And dominations, principalities and powers,
are delegated to witness
And declare the glory of before the Lord of
everything that is.
Of these great beings and mirrors of being,
little at present is known.

The "limits of your vision in time and number forbid you to
discriminate. . . ."
    The speaker then enumerates various ways of account-
ing for "these great beings and mirrors of being," but the
voice persists that little is known about "the manner of their
perceiving." They may not be as we imagine them at all.
Physics concentrates on the particulars of grains of sand and
the eccentricities of snowflakes. The historical point of view
"reckons and records the tides of time." Biology "Reads in
the chromatin Its cryptic scripture as the cell divides," and
mathematics considers such matters as probability and
chance in the order of things. All of this "counting without
confusion" is going on while what else is occurring?

                . . . while the pyramids stand still
In the desert and the deermouse huddles in
    his hold and the rain falls
Piercing the skin of the pool with water in
    water and making a million
And a million designs to be pleasingly latticed
    and laced and interfused
And mirrored to the Lord of everything that
    is by one and one and one.

In a way this expression of man's perception of reality is similar to the Zen parable of the reflection of the moonlight on the waves of the water. Depending on one's perspective, the picture appears differently, but after all, it is the same moon. But with this Nemerovian parable, there is perhaps not the same confidence. Somehow the pyramid seems quite impervious, the deermouse huddles in his hole quite undetected, and the very stuff of reality continues to feed "into itself" (or maybe from a source outside itself) and changes the very "transactions / Of all the particles."

What is the final effect of the poem? Certainly the "partialness" of vision is there, but perhaps the effect is not altogether one of despair. The poet began by saying "it is hard to imagine what life must be like," but when the poem is finished the vision of the world has become more inclusive because it images the sense of change and process with humility, and this sense of humility permits the flow of the mind to mingle with the flow of being.

The short poem "Knowledge," in *Gnomes & Occasions,* contains similar thematic ideas.

Not living for each other's sake,
Mind and the world will rarely rime;
The raindrops aiming at the lake
Are right on target every time.

The first two lines echo the idea in "Angel and Stone," that there are great limits to knowing. The last two lines are close in idea and feeling to the last two of "Angel and Stone": "And mirrored to the Lord of everything that is by one and one and one." Somehow, too, the intuition contained in both endings goes beyond paraphrase to a stillness, and a stillness where the reader resides.

Humility is further apparent in the first poem of that admirable sequence, "Runes" (*NSP*). It is a significant example of one side of Nemerov's art and evidence of his relevance to modern readers.

> This is about the stillness in moving things,
> In running water, also in the sleep
> Of winter seeds, where time to come has tensed
> Itself, enciphering a script so fine
> Only the hourglass can magnify it, only
> The years unfold its sentence from the root.
> I have considered such things often, but
> I cannot say I have thought deeply of them:
> That is my theme, of thought and the defeat
> Of thought of something and the thought of thought,
> A trader doubly burdened, commercing
> Out of one stillness and into another.

With the many references to mirrors and reflected images, it might be expected that the camera should figure in the poetry. In the "Sightseers" (*BS*) tourists walk about photographing "Where history was." One of the many "sights" recorded is the "Fathers" in the Badlands, and the speaker declares that "Sometimes they dream / Of looking alive," of entering the world of the living. But the camera, does not permit this:

> . . . reflexion
> Has intervened, and
> The dark will won
> Again, in the box
> That knows no now,
> In the mind bowed down
> Among the shadows
> Of shadowy things,
> Itself a shadow
> Less sure than they.

The reflected and static image of the "Fathers" has "intervened" in the dark of the box camera, which only knows the "past" and registers this in the blacks and whites of shadows

and is in a sense a shadow of the "real." By analogy, the
dream of looking alive was created by the power of the
imagination, but reflection intervened and "The dark will
won / Again." There is a fruitful association, in addition,
with the dark of the coffin in this box that knows no now.
The mind that reflects on the past and death and on the
death of the past has bowed its head among the shadows of
shadowy things; as a consequence this mind is less sure of its
own reality than the reality of things.

"In the Black Museum" (*BS*) is a dark poem themati-
cally and structurally. The darkness comes from a locked-in
system or structure when two mirrors face each other:

> Or as two mirrors vacuum-locked together
> Exclude, along with all the world,
> A light to see it by. Reflect on that.

In the earlier *Mirrors and Windows,* the arrangement of the
poems resembles in a larger way the structure of "In the
Black Museum." But the resemblance is only apparent. *Mirrors and Windows* opens with the poem "The Mirror" in
which the *persona* asks "how should I understand / What
happens here as in the other world. . .?" What intervenes or
stands between this question and the first mirror of the
book's beginning and the last mirror of the book's end is the
imagination and reflecting light of the poet, who is himself
using the mirror of language. The closing poem, and another
mirror, is *one* of the Nemerovian answers.

Holding the Mirror Up to Nature

> Some shapes cannot be seen in a glass
> those are the ones the heart breaks at.
> They will never become valentines
> or crucifixes, never. Night clouds
> go on insanely as themselves
> though metaphors would be prettier;

and when I see them massed at the edge
of the globe, neither weasel nor whale,
as though this world were, after all,
non-representational, I know
a truth that cannot be told, although
I try to tell you, "We are alone,
we know nothing, nothing, we shall die
frightened in our freedom, the one
who survives will change his name
to evade the vengeance for love. . . ."
Meanwhile the clouds go on clowning
over our heads in the floodlight of
a moon who is known to be Artemis
and Cynthia but sails away anyhow
beyond the serious poets with their
crazy ladies and cloudy histories,
their heroes in whose idiot dreams
the buzzard circles like a clock.

There are some "hard sayings" in this poem. In the world the night clouds do not resemble weasels and whales, do not "symbolize" or represent any underlying reality but "go on insanely as themselves." This is a "non-representational world." The moon once was Artemis or Cynthia, but as in "The Loon's Cry," it has fallen from the "symboled world." The "shapes" that are part of the human reality cannot be seen in a mirror, but these are the ones that break our hearts. In mid-poem Nemerov sadly concludes that man is solitary and that he knows nothing, and all the while, time, death's instrument, runs on. Such a poem has no doubt led to Meinke's description of Nemerov as a poet of "minimal affirmation." The poem also signifies that the important knowledge for the poet is *human* knowledge.

Two other poems allude to seminal myths in western thought and convey a poignant attitude toward the human problem of trying to see. "Beyond the Pleasure Principle" (*BS*) opens with a description of the beginnings of human thought in terms of the Beowulf story: just as Grendel and Grendel's mother may well mythicize or project man's early search for ways to handle fears of the unknown, or at least of terrifying forces, so does thought in general spring from such sources.

The second stanza continues this idea, alluding to various myth fragments, and especially to that one relating to the minotaur and the labyrinth.

> Our human thought arose at first in myth,
> And going far enough became a myth once more;
> Its pretty productions in between, those splendid
> Tarnhelms and winged sandals, mirroring shields
> And swords unbreakable, of guaranteed
> Fatality, those endlessly winding labyrinths
> In which all minotaurs might find themselves at
>   home,
> Deceived us with false views of the end, leaving
> Invisible the obstinate residuum, so cloudly, cold,
> Archaic, that waits beyond both purpose and
>   fulfillment.

Truly between theology and metaphysics alone, there are enough endless labyrinths for any and all minotaurs. But Nemerov observes that just as human thought was born in myth, so it returns, creating "pretty productions" that deceive us about the end.

But the sophisticated speaker admits something that yet remains a mystery for him, too. That even with the courage to ignore these "pretty productions" there remains "A something primitive and appealing, and still dangerous, / That crawls on bleeding hands and knees over the floor / Toward him, and whispers as if to confess: *again, again.*"

A different kind of mystery is intrinsic to the opening poem of *Gnomes & Occasions.* The very title, "Quaerendo Invenietis," conveys the state of chance that surrounds the attempt to learn about the world and the way out of our various labyrinths: in seeking to learn, you discover by chance.

I

I am the combination to a door
That fools and wise with equal ease undo.
Your unthought thoughts are changes still unread
In me, without whom nothing's to be said.

II

It is a spiral way that trues my arc
Toward central silence and my unreached mark.
Singing and saying till his time be done,
The traveler does nothing. But the road goes on.

III

Without my meaning nothing, nothing means.
I am the wave for which the worlds make way.
A term of time, and sometimes too of death,
I am the silence in the things you say.[9]

What one learns by chance is the crucial and pervasive nature of silence and nothing. That silence and nothing may be the mother of meaning, a twist to the well-known paradox that death is the mother of beauty: "Without my meaning nothing, nothing means." And the poet urges the reader to listen to the silences. Truly Nemerov is a poet of the silences, in all their terrifying aspects.

The closing poem of *Gnomes & Occasions* is yet another comment about the human adventure of seeking and learning. It is called "Beginner's Guide" and reveals the bewilderment one encounters in trying to learn about the physical world—the flowers, the birds, and the stars. The character in

9. Julia Bartholomay (in *The Shield of Perseus: The Vision and Imagination of Howard Nemerov*) remarks that Nemerov has divulged the answers to these riddles in public lectures: I, the alphabet; II, the tone-arm moving across the record; III, a sentence.

the poem buys field books to flowers and "Every spring he'd
tear / From their hiding-places, press and memorize / A
dozen pale beginners of the year." Summer comes, however,
and inundates him with species. His study of birds is even
more troubled, because flowers stand still at least. He concentrates on "sedentary birds" but they too are just as likely to
leave.

> The world would not, nor he could not, stand still.
> The longest life might be too short a one
> To get by heart, in all its fine detail,
> Earth's billion changes swinging on the sun.

His study of the stars was overwhelming. Hoping he would
get some help, he buys a telescope, but this only serves to
increase the number of stars to learn. The poem does not
stop on this note, however. It ends affirming the value of
learning as a continuing adventure.

> The world was always being wider
> And deeper and wiser than his little wit,
>
> But it felt good to know the hundred names
> And say them, in the warm room, in the winter,
> Drowsing and dozing over his trying times,
> Still to this world its wondering beginner.

"To a Scholar in the Stacks" (BS) takes up again the
labyrinth and the minotaur that was evident in "Beyond the
Pleasure Principle" and is more distinctly affirmative about
the pursuit of knowledge. It, incidentally, evidences a man of
letters in his late forties who has spent his adult life with
belles lettres. The poem opens by describing how the scholar
began his long journey in search of wisdom, the past, and
beauty. The "maze" of all the learning, its complexity,
seemed not even to offer an entrance. "A heart less bold

would have refused to start, / A mind less ignorant would have stayed home." All the action had been completed: Pasiphaë had borne the Minotaur, Daedalus had designed the labyrinth, and Theseus had found his way in and out of it many times. "What was there that had not been always done?" But because the scholar began, the way to the maze did open, and the story did become known.

> And now? You have gone down, you have gone in,
> You have become incredibly rich and wise
> From wandering underground. And yet you weary
> And disbelieve, daring the Minotaur
> Who answers in the echoes of your voice,
> Holding the thread that has no other end,
> Speaking her name whom you abandoned long ago.
>
> Then out of this what revelation comes?
> Sometimes in darkness and in deep despair
> You will remember, Theseus, that you were
> The Minotaur, the Labyrinth and the thread
> Yourself; even you were that ingener
> That fled the maze and flew—so long ago—
> Over the sunlit sea to Sicily.

This is a moving testimony and statement of belief by a scholar and man of letters in a time not especially noted for either moving testimonies or belief. It may well be that man himself has created the mazes and minotaurs, the devils and most intricate guilts. But just as surely, Nemerov says, he has found his way out and flown "Over the sunlit sea to Sicily."

The poems examined in this chapter demonstrate over and over that it is "human knowledge" that Nemerov engages. It is not his desire, or his error, to seek the "dehumanized" knowledge of naive realism or scientism. But Nemerov goes beyond merely letting the "things" speak for themselves ("To the things themselves") as "pure" phenomenology might demand. "Interpreting" bare things is alien to "pure" phenomenology, but not to the way of the poet. Like

students and philosophical descendants of Husserl, Nemerov
does not dwell on the method of knowing (as Husserl did),
but rather what the way of knowing might reveal. Nemerov
as poet has done what someone like Heidegger, Husserl's
student, has done as philosopher—to be primarily interested
in revealing "the stillness in moving things." It is to Heidegger
that I shall often turn to put Nemerov's world in a context.

2

"Running and standing still at once is the whole truth"

A sense of time and space is manifested in the poems to be examined in this chapter, and also a sense of the relatedness of things, which may be put into perspective by referring to two prominent twentieth-century analyses of such subjects, those of Whitehead and Heidegger. I think neither philosopher would agree with the other about how one should understand space and time, and space-time, but at points their conclusions resemble each other. This resemblance may be superficial (it occurs from different epistemological positions), but I include Whitehead's description for the perspective it puts on certain poems and, additionally, because Nemerov has referred to Whitehead numerous times in his own critical work. The parallel in the thinking of Nemerov and Heidegger manifests itself particularly in expressions of the nature of being. Both speak of the "stillness in moving things," the silence, the secret that language will never ultimately disclose.

The difference in Whitehead's and Heidegger's analyses of time has to do partly with their epistemological starting points. From Heidegger's starting point, time—as it has any authentic meaning for man—is finite. Infinite time may be metaphysically possible, but it would not be available or important to us.[1] From Whitehead's view, infinite time is not only possible, but in ways, describable.

Another difference in the metaphysical views of the two philosophers pertains to the kind of unity they see as pos-

1. For a discussion of this matter see Michael Gelven, *A Commentary on Heidegger's BEING AND TIME* (New York: Harper & Row, 1970), especially the part on the last two sections of *Being and Time*.

sible. While both men assert that any event enters into the being of every other event, that there is in a very real sense a relatedness to things, nowhere can I find in Heideggerian ontology a sense of meliorism inherent in process, a position which I think is fair to attribute to Whitehead. Thus it is to Whitehead's work that I will turn initially, to give perspective and additional light to certain poems of Nemerov that I believe share this view.

Many of Nemerov's best poems make statements about the unity and diversity of the world, and about the relationship of the mind to this world. Seven individual poems and a sequence of poems, "Runes," are taken up here because of their particular relevance to these essentially metaphysical considerations.

The speaker in "Painting a Mountain Stream" (*MW*) is answering the question, "How does one paint a mountain stream?" The beginning of the answer, and of the poem, makes some observations about the stream:

> Running and standing still at once
> is the whole truth. Raveled or combed,
> wrinkled or clear, it gets its force
> from losing force. Going it stays.
>
> Pulse beats, and planets echo this,
> the running down, the standing still,
> all thunder of the one thought.
> The mind that thinks it is unfounded.

The answer finally includes the recommendation: "paint this rhythm, not this thing."

Throughout the poem numerous paradoxes are introduced. How does the stream run and stand still? How does something get its force from losing force, or by going, stay? We say that a stream is running, and it obviously does; on the other hand, the "stream," the *form* of the stream, remains. By "losing" force in its beginning, the running stream gains force.

Nemerov is here observing and describing a mystery that occupied men at least as early as the pre-Socratics and probably long before. How does one account for such disparities or paradoxes? Is reality permanent or is it in a constant state of change as it appears to be? Heraclitus, against those of the Eleatic School, asserted that change is the reality. Just as Nemerov has chosen a stream to express this, so did Heraclitus in his famous dictum, "One cannot step twice into the same river." Heraclitus perceived a unity in all things, a unity of opposites. Nemerov expresses this as a rhythm. He has made a similar statement in an essay, "The Swaying Form: A Problem in Poetry." "The universe itself, so far as we relate ourselves to it by the mind, may be not so much a meaning as a rhythm, a continuous articulation of question and answer, question and answer, a musical dialectic precipitating out moments of meaning which become distinct only as one wave does in a sea of waves."[2]

About "Painting a Mountain Stream" the poet has written: "Of the many appearances of this figure of water in my work, I have chosen one that seeks to set the nature of water in relation to human perception and human imagination."[3] In this poem, he says, he has "stressed the liberal virtues and neglected the conservative ones, scorning the solids of this world to praise its liquids. This is not the whole truth, for how could you tell the stream but by its rocky bed, the rocks directing the water how to flow, the water—much more slowly—shaping the rocks according to its flow: But maybe I put the accent where I do against this world which so consistently in politics, religion, even in art, even in science, worships the rocky monument achieved and scorns the spring, the rain cloud, and the spark fallen among the leaves."[4] Of course, the poet is discussing human perception, whereas we are discussing ontology. However, given the meaning *perception* seems to have for Nemerov, there is no separation. In addition, we have his observation that "the

2. Nemerov, *Poetry and Fiction: Essays,* 11.
    3. Howard Nemerov, *Reflexions on Poetry and Poetics* (New Brunswick: Rutgers University Press, 1972), 172.
    4. *Ibid.,* 173.

universe itself, so far as we relate ourselves to it by the mind"
may be a "rhythm."

There are a number of poems that seem to express this
idea of reality, and often enough in terms of water. In "Angel
and Stone" the world was compared to a pond of water:

> But if you drop a stone into a pool, and
>   observe the ripples
> Moving in circles successively out to the edges
>   of the pool and then
> Reflecting back and passing through the ones
>   which continue to come
> Out of the center over the sunken stone, you
>   observe it is pleasing.

The "rhythms" in this poem are not identical with the
"rhythms" alluded to in the essay, but the example may still
hold. The elemental mobile substance is analogous to the
entire, mobile substance of the water in the pond, but the
pond is in constant motion.

"The Breaking of Rainbows" (BS) again employs a
stream or water metaphor, but the poem may not at first
seem to bear immediately on the issue at hand.

> Oil is spilling down the little stream
> Below the bridge. Heavy and slow as blood,
> Or with an idiot's driveling contempt:
> The spectral film unfolding, spreading forth
> Prismatically in a breaking of rainbows,
> Reflective radiance, marble evanescence,
> It shadows the secret moves the water makes,
> Creeping upstream again, then prowling down,
> Sometimes asleep in the dull corners, combed
> As the deep grass is combed in the stream's abandon,
> And sometimes tearing open silently
> Its seamless fabric in momentary shapes
> Unlikened and nameless as the shapes of sky

That open with the drift of cloud, and close,
High in the lonely mountains, silently.
The curve and glitter of it as it goes
The maze of its pursuit, reflect the water
In agony under the alien, brilliant skin
It struggles to throw off and finally does
Throw off, on its frivolous purgatorial fall
Down to the sea and away, dancing and singing
Perpetual intercession for this filth—
Leaping and dancing and singing, forgiving everything.

This oily film serves as a mirror which reflects the constant change that takes place: "It shadows the secret moves the water makes." Concurrently, the oil film metaphor functions as something that is not beautiful, that is filth, and is associated with such unpleasantness as "an idiot's driveling contempt." What is important here is that the oil film is thrown off, or in fact assimilated, or transmuted. This stream of reality not only changes but seems to change for the better. The implications of "The Breaking of Rainbows," together with the evidence of poems to be analyzed subsequently, seem to point to an idea of reality and process that goes beyond a pure phenomenology.

It is here that Nemerov seems to hold a position that resembles Whitehead's. Armand Maurer makes the following remarks concerning Whitehead's "philosophy of organism," from which I must draw a somewhat extended passage as evidence:

An event occurs at some place and time, but not at a point in space or at an instant in time. . . . Each event is spread out over space and time and consequently it has spatial and temporal extension. . . . Another important characteristic of events is that they extend over each other. For example, the endurance of the Great Pyramid is an event that overlaps many goings-on of briefer duration in Egypt.

Every event, no matter how small its extension, extends over other events that are contained in it as parts, and it itself is contained
as a part of other events that extend over it.
Accordingly, the universe is a web or network
of events, each of which is a unit but intimately
connected with other events. This inter-
connection of events is not something external
to them, like the external relations between
bodies in mechanistic physics, or between
impressions in the philosophy of Hume;
the relations binding events together enter
in their very being, with the result that
events cannot be completely described without them. In this view, nature is an organic
unity in which every event has some bearing
on everything else. "Any local agitation
shakes the whole universe. The distant effects
are minute, but they are there." In a sense,
then, "everything is everywhere at all times.
For every location involves an aspect of itself
in every other location. Thus every spatio-
temporal standpoint mirrors the world."[5]

Because of this spatio-temporal interconnectedness of events,
prior events pass into subsequent ones and take part in the
creative advance of nature. Thus, the "philosophy of organism" is not to be construed to pertain only to the animal
and plant world, but includes what is commonly referred to
as "inorganic." It is Whitehead's position that the universe as
organism is moving in a purposeful direction. God "saves the
world as it passes into the immediacy of his own life. It is the
judgment of a tenderness which loses nothing that can be
saved. It is also the judgment of a wisdom which uses what in
the temporal world is mere wreckage."[6]

    5. Etienne Gilson, Thomas Langan, and Armand A. Maurer, *Recent
Philosophy, Hegel to the Present* (New York: Random House, 1966), 511–12.
Maurer wrote the section pertaining to Whitehead.
    6. *Ibid.,* 517.

　　In reference to a "judgment" that "uses what in the temporal world is mere wreckage," consider, for example, Nemerov's "The Breaking of Rainbows" and the oil film metaphor. Is not this a similar attitude concerning process and change? Heraclitus would likely explain the oil film as one of the necessary "opposites" that will be united in a dynamic process, and which is thus *essential* to reality. Nemerov's attitude is that the rhythm and energy of nature can somehow *overcome* even such a "wreckage."

　　As I said at the beginning of this chapter, Whitehead recognizes a relatedness of things, and this is an element often present in the work of Nemerov. Recall Maurer's statement of Whitehead's position: "The universe is a web or network of events, each of which is a unit but intimately connected with other events. . . . The relations binding events together enter into their very being, with the result that events cannot be completely described without them."[7] Or, in Whitehead's own words: "Any local agitation shakes the whole universe. The distant effects are minute, but they are there. . . . Everything is everywhere at all times. For every location involves an aspect of itself in every other location. Thus every spatio-temporal standpoint mirrors the world."[8] To return to "Painting a Mountain Stream":

> Pulse beats, and planets echo this,
> the running down, the standing still,
> all thunder of the one thought.

And of course the waves or ripples that result when the pond is agitated by a pebble move "in circles successively out to the edges of the pool and then / Reflecting back and passing through the ones which continue to come" ("Angel and Stone").

　　Certain elements of Nemerov's view appear to have an emphasis that is different from that of Whitehead, however.

---

7. *Ibid.*, 511.
8. *Ibid.*

One reason for this, I think, is Nemerov's preoccupation with the *human* present, the human sense of *now* (as in the poem "Moment," for example). This emphasis is not so strikingly apparent in Whitehead's sense of time, and Nemerov's view may perhaps be placed in clearer perspective by introducing Heidegger's words on the subject. Another justification for reference to Heidegger here is that his view of what underlies being and the language he uses to mirror this ground are very close to the ideas and language found in Nemerov's "Runes" sequence. To an extent, Nemerov's view may be said to resonate between the idea of space-time as advanced in relativity theory, and the idea of time and space formulated in existential thinking.

There are several places in Heidegger's work where one might turn for his position concerning temporality and related matters; certainly *Being and Time* is a major statement (first published in 1927). But the brief essay, "The Nature of Language," (1958) will serve our purposes on this question and many others later in this study. A difficulty exists, especially in the instance of Heidegger, of isolating short passages wherein key words are used that have been defined (often at great length) in previous work. This risk will be taken, but with some attempt to point out the boundaries of such terms.

Heidegger notes that the calculating mind measures such conditions as nearness and remoteness in terms of the parameters of space and time, and these in turn as static distances (e.g., the methods of measurement in relativity and quantum theories). But the new theories of relativity and quantum mechanics have changed nothing in the parametrical character of space and time.

> If nearness and neighborliness could be conceived parametrically, then a distance of the magnitude of one millionth of a second, and of one millimeter, would have to mean the nearest possible neighboring nearness, compared with which even the distance of a yard and a minute represents extreme remoteness.

Even so, we are bound to insist that a certain spatial-temporal relatedness belongs to every neighborhood. Two isolated farmsteads—if any such are left—separated by an hour's walk across the fields, can be the best of neighbors, while two townhouses, facing each other across the street or even sharing a common wall, know no neighborhood. Neighboring nearness, then, does not depend on spatial-temporal relation. Nearness, then, is by its nature outside and independent of space and time. . . .

Where this prevails [this face-to-face relationship to people and gods, earth and sky] all things are open to one another in their self-concealment; thus one extends itself to the other, and thus all remain themselves; one is over the other as its guardian watching over the other, over it as its veil.[9]

Nighness is the word Heidegger gives to the "movement at the core of the world's four regions, which makes them reach one another and holds them in the nearness of their distance, is nearness itself. This movement is what paves the way for being face-to-face." Nearness in respect to this movement is *nighness;* and this movement

remains unapproachable, and is farthest from us whenever we talk "about" it. However, space and time as parameters can neither bring about nor measure nearness. Why not? In the succession of "nows" one after the other as elements of parametric time, one "now" is never in open face-to-face encounter with another. In fact, we may not even say

9. Martin Heidegger *On the Way to Language*, tr. Peter D. Hertz (New York: Harper & Row, 1971), 103.

that, in this succession, the "now" coming
after and the "now" coming before are closed
off from each other. For closure, too, is still a
manner of facing or excluding something
being in face-to-face. But this encounter is as
such excluded from the parametric concept of
time. . . .

Time times simultaneously: the has-been,
presence, and the present that is waiting for
our encounter and is normally called the future. Time in its timing removes us into its
threefold simultaneity, moves us thence while
holding out to us the disclosure of what is in
the same time, the concordant oneness of the
has-been, presence, and the present waiting
the encounter. In removing us and bringing
toward us, time moves on its way what simultaneity yields and throws open to it: time-
space. But time itself, in the wholeness of its
nature, does not move; it rests in stillness.
    The same is to be said about space: it
spaces, throws open locality and places, va-
cates them and at the same time gives them
free for all things and receives what is simultaneous as space-time. But space itself, in the
wholeness of its nature, does not move; it
rests in stillness.[10]

In these passages there are clear departures from the sense of
Now found in Whitehead's theory of organism. *Nearness* and
neighborhood take on their meaning outside relativity
theory. With these passages in the background, let us turn to
the poem "Moment" (*NSP*). A great deal of Nemerov's world
is intensely compacted in these fifteen lines:

10. *Ibid.*, 104, 106.

Now, starflake frozen on the windowpane
All of a winter night, the open hearth
Blazing beyond Andromeda, the sea-
Anemone and the downwind seed, O moment
Hastening, halting in a clockwise dust,
The time in all the hospitals is now,
Under the arc-lights where the sentry walks
His lonely wall it never moves from now,
The crying in the cell is also now,
And now is quiet in the tomb as now
Explodes inside the sun, and it is now
In the saddle of space, where argosies of dust
Sail outward blazing, and the mind of God,
The flash across the gap of being, thinks
In the instant absence of forever: now.

We perceive the scene In "Moment" through the intelligence situated between an open fire and a window that faces the winter night. The snowflake in the form of a star is frozen to the windowpane. The reflection of the fireplace seems to place its fiery glow beyond the constellation of Andromeda. Beyond Andromeda, astronomically, is the "fire" of the great spiral nebula M31. This is a moment in the clockwise turn of the constellations, which is also one expression of time. Time hastens and halts relative to the human scenes that follow. The sick, the imprisoned, and the dead all seem to be a part of the same fabric, a fabric at least held together by time, this moment, or *now*. "Crying in the cell" represents not only the cell of the prisoner, which the sentry guards, but also in some generative sense, crying of birth and the living, the cell as an organic unit, thus juxtaposing life and death.

Simultaneously, the sun of our own solar system explodes while stellar dust moves outward in an expanding universe, the "curved" universe of Einstein. The metaphor for the mind of God recalls the arc-lights under which the lonely figure of the sentry walks the wall around the cells. The mind of God is conceived in terms of a current of force like that which exists between two carbon rods, a current that leaps across the "gap of being." The poet, by opening himself to the world, intuits a relatedness of events. This intuition shares a resemblance to Whitehead's conception, but the human focus bears the emphasis that Heidegger describes, this face-to-face encounter that is excluded from the parametric concept of time. Or again, where this face-to-face relationship to people and gods, earth and sky exists, "all things are open to one another in their self-concealment; thus one extends itself to the other, and thus all remain themselves; one is over the other as its guardian watching over the other, over it as its veil."[11]

Although there are related clusters of events in the poem, there is at first a surface of arbitrariness: explosions in the sun, the quiet in the tomb, and the constellation Andromeda. But these have extension for Nemerov—a temporal extension in the Now, not apart from but concurrent with an idea of being as force that extends across and unifies the world.

"Moment" is a good example of what Miller Williams was talking about when he said that Nemerov had "carried on the search for a kind of unified field theory, some metaphor to bring time and space, being and non-being into harmony, and to say where and what man is in the reality and illusion of all this."[12]

"The Tapestry," from *Gnomes and Occasions* may serve as a kind of addendum and qualification to the consolation that the world is of a piece.

>On this side of the tapestry
>There sits the bearded king,
>And round about him stand
>His lords and ladies in a ring.
>His hunting dogs are there,
>And armed men at command.

11. *Ibid.*, 103.
12. Miller Williams, "Transactions with the Muse," *Saturday Review* (March 9, 1968), reprinted in Bowie Duncan (ed.), *The Critical Reception of Howard Nemerov*, 142–43.

On that side of the tapestry
The formal court is gone,
The kingdom is unknown;
Nothing but thread to see,
Knotted and rooted thread
Spelling a world unsaid.

Men do not find their way
Through a seamless maze,
And all direction lose
In a labyrinth of clues,
A forest of loose ends
Where sewing never mends.

The very "seamless" nature of the tapestry of the world thwarts the human exploration. In addition, men find themselves in a world that resembles the back side of a tapestry, thus left with a few "loose ends" or clues about what is on the other side (yes, there might be a "bearded king" on the other side, but on the other hand. . .).

"The Puzzle" and "Snowflakes," both from the same volume as "The Tapestry," further substantiate the evidence that this "minority report" about a world all of a piece but distressing to those who live in it is a view that has remained rather constant in Nemerov's work. In the instance of "The Puzzle," children are at work putting together a picture puzzle of a desert scene which includes the Pyramids and the Sphinx. They are "rebuilding the continuum from its bits" but when they have completed this picture of the world, they complete "the vision of a ruined world." In the poem "Snowflakes" a blind energy seems to find completion also in that which is fallen or ruined.

Not slowly wrought, nor treasured for their form
In heaven, but by the blind self of the storm
Spun off, each driven individual
Perfected in the moment of his fall.

"Lines & Circularities" (*G&O*) reflects a model of the world that is of a piece and continuous in the way of a spiraling phonograph record. The occasion for the poem is, as the subtitle tells us, "on hearing Casals' recording of the Sixth Suite." The world of the spiraling record reflects the attribute of time.

> Deep in a time that cannot come again
> Bach thought it through, this lonely and immense
> Reflexion wherein our sorrows learn to dance.
> And deep in the time that cannot come again
> Casals recorded it.

As the speaker listens he watches the tone-arm

> enact
> A mystery wherein the music shares:
> How time, that comes and goes and vanishes
> Never to come again, can come again.

Through artifice, imagination, time comes again. The speaker has the past remembered for him. The needle of the tone-arm follows "through winding ways to silence at the close; the delicate needle" follows the edges of the spiral, the small striations that reflect the master's mind.

The poem then shifts to a consideration of the earth that spins on itself, like the record, and of the sun that swings its satellites around itself as it, too, moves about the turning galaxy. Increasingly in the later volumes, it is evident that the curve and spiral of the Einsteinian model of the world has excited the imagination of Nemerov and served him well as analogy for his own vision.

Presently some astronomers debate whether the universe will always expand, or whether it may perhaps reverse itself and contract. This oscillation may go on eternally, or it might do as the poet's record player does in the conclusion of the poem.

The music dances to its inner edge
And stops. The tone-arm lifts and cocks its head
An instant, as if listening for something
That is no longer there but might be; then
Returns to rest, as with a definite click
The whole strange business turns itself off.

What I would like to call attention to (and what the poem calls attention to) is "the winding ways to silence," and the "listening for something / That is no longer there but might be." There is a great deal of listening in the poetry of Nemerov, and much listening to stillness (about which I will have more to say in Chapter 4). In the "Runes" sequence, which I will turn to shortly, stillness again is very much the subject. How are we to understand this stillness? Recall the last passage that was quoted from Heidegger's "The Nature of Language." There he asserted that time and space, in the wholeness of their natures, do not move; they rest in stillness. Bearing in mind what has been said of Heidegger's sense of time earlier in this chapter, consider what Nemerov may mean, when he speaks of stillness, in the light of this passage from Heidegger:

> Mortals are they who can experience death as death. Animals cannot do so. But animals cannot speak either. The essential relation between death and language flashes up before us, but remains still unthought. It can, however, beckon us toward the way in which the nature of language draws us into its concern and so relates us to itself, in case death belongs together with what reaches out for us, touches us. . . .
>
> Saying, as the way-making movement of the world's fourfold, gathers all things up into the nearness of face-to-face encounter, and does so soundlessly, as quietly as time times, space spaces, as quietly as the play of time-space is enacted.

> The soundless gathering call, by which
> Saying moves the world-relation on its way,
> we call the ringing of stillness. It is: the lan-
> guage of being.[13]

This is the nature of the stillness that Nemerov speaks of in
"Lines & Circularities" and which we will see he speaks of in
"Runes": this stillness is the language of being.

Nemerov has written two sequences of short poems, the
earlier one called "The Scales of the Eyes" (included first in
The Salt Garden) and the later sequence entitled simply
"Runes," which follows the short poem "Moment" in his
New and Selected Poems. In the first sequence Nemerov has
journeyed inward to know himself. Kenneth Burke, who
has examined the sequence at length, writes that "The
poet has gone into a huddle with himself, to ask emphatically
about the essence of himself, which in turn is seen in terms of
his vocation."[14] The journey results in a new vision as the
scales might be said to fall from his eyes.

If the direction of "The Scales of the Eyes" is principally inward, the direction of "Runes" is outward from the
self to a world of change, of diversity, but a world that
includes an element of permanence. An inscription from St.
Augustine is overture to the tensions and paradoxes that load
the fifteen-poem sequence: " . . . insaniebam salubriter et
moriebar vitaliter," a translation of which might be, "I was
going insane healthy, and I was dying full of life." "Runes" I
take literally to mean secrets and mysteries. To suggest the
ruins that are part of his subject in this sequence, Nemerov
puns in the first poem (quoted in full on page 23) on the
"stillness in moving things." He announces here (and it may
not be insignificant that the first poem has only fourteen
lines instead of fifteen, perhaps suggesting that the "secret" is
missing)[15] the subject of the whole "Runes" sequence. The

---

13. Heidegger, *On the Way to Language,* 107–108.

14. Kenneth Burke, "Comments on Eighteen Poems by Howard Nemerov,"
Sewanee Review, LX (January, 1952), 129.

15. Bartholomay, *The Shield of Perseus,* 114. Mrs. Bartholomay suggests
the subtitle is incorporated in Rune 1. The reader is directed to her extensive discussion of the "Runes."

poet echoes what we have heard about time in "Painting a Mountain Stream," but this poem suggests a more limited aspect of time, "the sleep / Of winter seeds, where time to come has tensed / Itself." As he has tried to think of such mysteries and paradoxes, his attempts to explain the mysteries or resolve the paradoxes have been defeated: "That is my theme, of thought and the defeat / Of thought before its object, where it turns / As from a mirror, and returns to be / The thought of something and the thought of thought, / A trader doubly burdened, commercing / Out of one stillness and into another." Nemerov concludes that his attempts themselves seem to be like turning from a mirror (whereupon the "object" disappears), thinking about perception itself, returning to consider the object in the mirror, and being doubly burdened.

Several images anticipate or commence the development of the themes of reality-in-flux and its relation to time: a stillness-movement cluster, running water, seeds, and trading imagery. Rune II picks up the first of these as it ponders the story of Ulysses. In Homer's account the hero returns to Ithaca and remains in a manner at rest. Dante's account would have it the other way, with Ulysses "beyond the gates" and sailing south. The poet concludes that he does not know the right one. Thus we are left with the mystery of the first poem: how is it that things seem to move and yet are still, or vice versa?

Rune III takes up seed-growth and trading imagery.

> Sunflowers, traders rounding the horn of time
> Into deep afternoons, sleepy with gain,
> The fall of silence has begun to storm
> Around you where you nod your heavy heads
> Whose bare poles, raking out of true, will crack,
> Driving your wreckage on the world's lee shore.
> Your faces no more will follow the sun,
> But bow down to the ground with a heavy truth
> That dereliction learns, how charity
> Is strangled out of selfishness at last;
> When, golden misers in the courts of summer,
> You are stripped of gain for coining images

And broken on this quarter of the wheel,
It is on savage ground you spill yourselves,
And spend the tarnished silver of your change.

The "time to come has tensed," of Rune I, here takes on more meaning in the figure of the sunflowers. The sunflowers are compared to "traders rounding the horn of time" because of their characteristic of facing the rising sun and then slowly turning westward as the sun does (time and light moving, one moving on and the other, out). There is an oblique continuation of Ulysses-sailor in the daring trader moving around the horn. There may be an undercurrent of pun in "trader" to traitor. The sunflowers are not the traitors, but they are about to be betrayed or robbed. Maybe their indolence and greed ("sleepy with gain") cause them to betray themselves. Thus, the image of opulence, fertility and completeness, begins to erode after "The fall of silence has begun to storm" such riches. The tone shifts rapidly and the sound-sense harmony of "sun-deep-gain" becomes harsher with the bleakness of "whose bare poles, raking out of true, will crack." The conceit is continued as the traders drive the wreckage of their ships on the shore, specifically "the world's lee shore." Besides the ironic meaning of wrecking on the sheltered shore, there is the other meaning of "lee," that is as a sediment, or a dreg, an image which develops the theme of a loss of fertility and growth. The lee shore then is the dry shore where the derelict is left, high and dry. Charity strangled out of selfishness becomes additionally charged with meaning as the derelict ship is a "gift" to anyone who finds or claims it. This is a heavy truth, the poet says. The trader-ship is stripped of the gold for making coins; the sunflowers are stripped of their seeds. The sunflowers may be said to "coin images" in at least two ways: the seeds will obviously coin new images of the sunflower, and in a punitive sense, the sunflower is being stripped perhaps for coining an image of the sun. It is being "broken on this quarter of the wheel" which would be the quarter of the year's turning, summer. The trader-ship is broken on the savage ground and spills what is left, the "tarnished silver." The sunflower has through its change from one state to another, spilled its seeds on the ground. The predominant tone of this poem is, of course, not of fertility, but of loss of fertility, or at best a tarnished or failed fertility. What happens very subtly at the end of the poem drives one back through it again because of the resonances of "spilling or spending" seeds on the ground. Although ironic, the sexual overtones of this image counterpoint the images of growth, fertility, and death of the sunflower. Lines increase this complexity and density: " . . . you nod your heavy heads / Whose bare poles, raking out of true, will crack . . . Your faces no more will follow the sun, / But bow down to the ground with a heavy truth . . . You are stripped of gain for coining images." And of course it was for this reason that Onan spilt his seed on the ground when he slept with his sister-in-law Tamar: "But Onan knew that the issue would not be his," or that he had been stripped of gain for coining images.

Rune IV might be considered as a micro-drama of the birth of evil.

> The seed sleeps in the furnaces of death,
> A cock's egg slept till hatching by a serpent
> Wound in his wintry coil, a spring so tight
> In his radical presence that every tense
> Is now. Out of this head the terms of kind,
> Distributed in syntax, come to judgment,
> Are basilisks who write our sentences
> Deep at the scripture's pith, in rooted tongues,
> How one shall marry while another dies.
> Give us our ignorance, the family tree
> Grows upside down and shakes its heavy fruit,
> Whose buried stones philosophers have sought.
> For each stone bears the living word, each word
> Will be made flesh, and all flesh fall to seed:
> Such stones from the tree; and from the stones,
>   such blood.

This poem begins with an idea that has held the attention of poets rather persistently, and in particular one of Nemerov's contemporaries, Dylan Thomas; "The Force That Through the Green Fuse Drives the Flower" and even "Altar-wise by Owl-Light" express these themes. The beginning of life is the beginning of death. Likewise, there was no life until there was death. And biblically, there was no death until there was evil; thus, "A cock's egg slept till hatching by a serpent / Wound in his wintry coil." I presume "A cock's egg" is expressive of God's creation of man. This is similar to "Old cock from nowheres and the heaven's egg" of the poem "Altarwise by Owl-Light." "A spring so tight / In his radical presence that every tense / Is now" may mean, besides the literal spring-like coils tightening around man, that in the spring (or beginning) that emerges from this winter there is something in the *root* presence (existing inherently in this presence) that makes every grammatical tense in the now, or present. (Note, also, how this returns to the "root" of line six in Rune I).

Out of this evil come the terms of likeness and difference, of gender and sex, of birth, race and species, distributed in the language of order and the order of language (syntax), and with perhaps a pun on syntax, *i.e.,* "sin-tax." Out of this head come the terms of judgment and the basilisks who "write our sentences": ambiguously, the sentences of language and the decree on the convicted. Such paradoxical sentences are written and handed out that while "one shall marry," form union, and create, "another dies."

Parodying the Lord's Prayer, "Give us our ignorance," the poet goes on to say that "the family tree / Grows upside down and shakes its heavy fruit," or, instead of the tree growing toward life and sun and generation, it is upside down, growing toward death. "The heavy fruit" is shaken off to die and has buried within it the stone that philosophers seek—the stone that will unlock the secret of the universe. The secret found in this "living word" is that of death, reinforced perhaps by the "burial stone" association. "All flesh fall to seed," or die. This is the kind of pain-and-death fruit that springs from this Tree of Life.

Rune V continues the mysterious nature of seed through the language of the harvest. What also might be noted aside here is the feeling for ancient Hebraic history and life that often appears in Nemerov's work.

The fat time of the year is also time
Of the Atonement; birds to the berry bushes,
Men to the harvest; a time to answer for
Both present plenty and emptiness to come.
When the slain legal deer is salted down,
When apples smell like goodness, cold in the cellar,
You hear the ram's horn sounded in the high
Mount of the Lord, and you lift up your eyes
As though by this observance you might hide
The dry husk of an eaten heart which brings
Nothing to offer up, no sacrifice
Acceptable but the canceled-out desires
And satisfactions of another year's
Abscess, whose zero in His winter's mercy
Still hides the undecipherable seed.

Harvest time, the poet tells us, is also the time of Atonement, a time of union, of becoming "at-one" with God; but Atonement is also a day of fasting, and a day for sacrificing the bull, the ram, and the scapegoat. This is the way to redemption through propitiation, (as Christ was to redeem man by becoming scapegoat later in Jewish history). Thus, the dual nature of the harvest is already foreshadowed. This will be a time for "Both present plenty and emptiness to come."

The speaker here confesses that for him the Atonement is a kind of subterfuge whereby he can "hide / The dry husk of an eaten heart which brings / Nothing to offer up." His husk of a heart has no acceptable sacrifice except desires that have cancelled themselves out and satisfactions of sins that have abscessed his flesh. At the poem's end, the "zero" of his sacrifice still does not understand the mystery of life and the seed, "the stillness in moving things" that was announced in the beginning of the sequence.

The motif of winter is continued in Rune VI, with moving water trapped in the stillness of a winter's prison. Madness and insanity are associated with snow.

White water now in the snowflake's prison,
A mad king in a skullcap thinks these thoughts
In regular hexagons, each one unlike

Each of the others. The atoms of memory,
Like those that Democritus knew, have hooks
At either end, but these? Insane tycoon,
These are the riches of order snowed without end
In this distracted globe, where is no state
To fingerprint the flakes or number these
Moments melting in flight, seeds mirroring
Substance without position or a speed
And course unsubstanced. What may the spring be,
Deep in the atom, among galactic snows,
But the substance of things hoped for, argument
Of things unseen? White water, fall and fall.

The dissimilarity of things is emphasized and trader-merchant
become "Insane tycoon" in this poem. "These are the riches
of order snowed without end / In this distracted globe." In
a curious line, the seeds in this winter have become snowflakes: "seeds mirroring / Substance without position or a
speed / And course unsubstanced." This seems to recall the
idea of mass and light of Einsteinian physics. The "seeds"
reflect the substance not in a fixed position (in other words,
only relative position) and a speed and direction that has no
substance, like light. This recalls the description of Whitehead's view, also, that "An event occurs at some place and
time, but not at a point in space or at an instant in time." [16]
The poem ends with a question and a hesitant, tentative
answer. "What may the spring be, / Deep in the atom,
among galactic snows, / But the substance of things hoped
for, argument / Of things unseen?" The answer echoes
Paul's consolation to the Hebrews (11:1) where he writes,
"Now faith is the substance of things hoped for, the evidence
of things not seen." Spring figures at first in two ways: the
season of spring that will emerge from this winter, and the
force of a spring lying deep within fundamental atomic
substance. But, recalling from Rune IV the "spring" of line
three, there is the association of evil that further enriches the
ending of Rune VI and looks forward to the end of the
sequence.

16. Gilson, Langan, and Maurer, *Recent Philosophy*, 511.

Rune VII opens with the words of Jacob to his son Reuben.

> Unstable as water, thou shalt not excel[17]
> —Said to the firstborn, the dignity and strength,
> And the defiler of his father's bed.
> Fit motto for a dehydrated age
> Nervously watering whisky and stock,
> Quick-freezing dreams into realities.
> Brain-surgeons have produced the proustian syndrome,
> But patients dunk their tasteless madeleines
> In vain, those papers that the Japanese
> Amused themselves by watering until
> They flowered and became Combray, flower
> No more. The plastic and cosmetic arts
> Unbreakably record the last word and
> The least word, till sometimes even the Muse,
> In her transparent raincoat, resembles a condom.

The speaker says that Jacob's words are a fit motto for this dehydrated, or unfertile, age. Instead of fertility, a creative act, the age is "watering whisky," deviously making it less potent, and watering stock, which is not *real* increase, but only additional shares. Brain-surgeons produce the "proustian syndrome," of total inwardness, but these patients do not remember the past. Plastic, unbreakable phonograph records record without creative selection "the last word and / The least word," and the Muse begins to "resemble a condom," which also unbreakably "records," or "preserves," the last and least of the living "words" in genetic language. The irony of this recalls the first line of the poem, "thou shalt not excel," with "excel" having phallic overtones of "to rise above," or "to raise, as columns." Thus, midway in the sequence the seeds are not ending finally in life, but in a futile dead end.

17. Genesis 49:3,4. Reuben, thou art my firstborn, my might, and the beginning of my strength, the excellency of power. Unstable as water, thou shalt not excel; because thou wentest up to thy father's bed; then defiledst it; he went up to my couch.

Runes VIII and IX continue to explore water as a force that moves downward, to death and to ruin. In Rune VIII the water is followed down ditches, under culverts, through swamps, and ultimately to "The dog's corpse in the ditch, to come at last / Into the pit where zero's eye is closed." Rune IX enumerates more facets of "this dehydrated time." Men "Bottle holy water / In plastic tears, and bury mustard seeds / In lucite lockets."

In the tenth poem, the riddle of the white, rushing water is still not clear. "Your utterance is riddled." But the speaker concludes from watching what the falling water does, how

> . . . history is no more than
> The shadows thrown by clouds on mountainsides,
> A distant chill, when all is brought to pass
> By rain and birth and rising of the dead.

The tensions of seed and death call up the examples of Aaron, Jesse, Adam and the Son of Man in Rune XI.

> A holy man said to me, "Split the stick
> And there is Jesus." When I split the stick
> To the dark marrow and the splintery grain
> I saw nothing that was not wood, nothing
> That was not God, and I began to dream
> How from the tree that stood between the rivers
> Came Aaron's rod that crawled in front of Pharaoh,
> And came the rod of Jesse flowering
> In all the generations of the Kings,
> And came the timbers of the second tree,
> The sticks and yardarms of the holy three-
> masted vessel whereon the Son of Man
> Hung between thieves, and came the crown of thorns,
> The lance and ladder, when was shed that blood
> Streamed in the grain of Adam's tainted seed.

When told to contemplate the marrow or pith of a stick to learn its mysteries, the dreams of Aaron's rod, a symbol of authority for the family of Israel; it becomes a serpent also, when thrown at Pharaoh's feet. He thinks of the rod of Jesse, father of David, as the instrument for a long fertile line. But this happy thought quickly gives way to "the timbers of the second tree, / The sticks and yardarms of the holy three- / masted vessel," reviving one aspect of the sailor-trading cluster, this time commercing into the silence of the death of Christ. The blood of the crucified Christ joins the stream of blood that flows from Adam's tainted seed, the seed that since tainted contains sin and death.

One observes over and over in the body of Nemerov's poetry a vision of the relatedness of natural events; and though events occur "by one and one and one," yet there is a unified fabric, either in terms of the "rhythm" that he often speaks of, or a sense of some elemental unifying force or energy that leaps the "gap of being." Equipped with such a vision, he habitually reflects a compacted world in his poetry, and, though not as a necessary consequence, his poetry reflects that world in a compacted language. Rune XII is additional evidence.

> Consider how the seed lost by a bird
> Will harbor in its branches most remote
> Descendants of the bird; while everywhere
> And unobserved, the soft green stalks and tubes
> Of water are hardening into wood, whose hide,
> Gnarled, knotted, flowing, and its hidden grain,
> Remember how the water is streaming still.
> Now does the seed asleep, as in a dream
> Where time is compacted under pressures of
> Another order, crack open like stone
> From whose division pours a stream, between
> The raindrop and the sea, running in one
> Direction, down, and gathering in its course
> That bitter salt which spices us the food
> We sweat for, and the blood and tears we shed.

What seems to be true in this poem, and in others, is an idea of individual death, a death that returns an entity to the stream of reality, but a confidence that the stream and rhythm of the universe will continue to ebb and flow, and this is affirmation. This is part of the Nemerovian world picture that takes it beyond the "minimal affirmation" that Meinke has hypothesized. In his monograph, Meinke singles out Rune XII as an example of Nemerov's "impeccable style." He says further:

> The water streaming in the seed streams through our world, our bodies, holding everything together in its always-changing permanence. The subtle rhythms support the imagery in a fusion of form and content; run-ons, alliteration, repetition, all playing important roles in the structure. The "s" sound in "soft green stalks and tubes," the "d" sound in "hardening into wood, whose hide, / Gnarled, knotted" reinforce the meaning; the rhythm, stopped by "whose hide, / Gnarled, knotted," flows forward again with "Flowing, and its hidden grain." The end of the first sentence holds the paradox of permanent impermanence in the ambiguous "streaming still." The onomatopoeic "crack" splits the second sentence, whose alliteration and longer phrases ("gathering in its course / That bitter salt which spices us the food / We sweat for") underline the stanza's conclusion.[18]

The poem restates the notion of time that has pervaded the sequence. This time is relative to another perspective and therefore to another order.

The theme of trader and commerce is taken up with a vengeance in Rune XIII. At the same time, the image clusters

18. Peter Meinke, *Howard Nemerov* (Minneapolis: University of Minnesota Press, 1968), 24–25.

around running water and the seed (now tainted with blood) and interweaves theme and structure.

> There sailed out on the river, Conrad saw,
> The dreams of men, the seeds of commonwealths,
> The germs of Empire. To the ends of the earth
> One many-veined bloodstream swayed the hulls
> Of darkness gone, of darkness still to come,
> And sent its tendrils steeping through the roots
> Of wasted continents. That echoing pulse
> Carried the ground swell of all sea-returns
> Muttering under history, and its taste,
> Saline and cold, was as a mirror of
> The taste of human blood. The sailor leaned
> To lick the mirror clean, the somber and
> Immense mirror that Conrad saw, and saw
> The other self, the sacred Cain of blood
> Who would seed a commonwealth in the Land of Nod.

This recalls the opening and closing scenes of *Heart of Darkness* where Marlow sits on a ship in the Thames as darkness comes on the river telling his story of colonial empire, greed, and murder. "Seeds" of commonwealths take on additional meaning in this rune, by now having been highly charged with the imagery of "seeds spent on the ground," a seed gripped so tight in evil's radical presence, and seeds that stream with blood. "Germs of Empire" are likewise germs of reproduction, but also disease-producing microbes. The "many-veined bloodstream" of men in quest for wealth and power, like King Leopold's company in the Congo, has "swayed the hulls / Of darkness" in the past, now, and in the time to come. The hulls are the hulls of the trader ships, but also the hull of the heart of Mister Kurtz, that heart full of horror, and further enrich "The dry husks of an eaten heart" of Rune V. The echoing pulse of the stream of greed tastes like the "taste of human blood." To lick this mirror of human blood is to see the other self, first offspring of Adam's tainted seed, "sacred Cain."[19] Thus the time to come that "has tensed / Itself" is slowly being unfolded toward an end that has been well prepared for.

Rune XIV is made of the language of thresholds, edges, tense membranes, all leading to a point just on the verge of falling apart.

> There is a threshold, that meniscus where
> The strider walks on drowning waters, or
> That tense, curved membrane of the camera's lens
> Which darkness holds against the battering light
> And the distracted drumming of the world's
> Importunate plenty.—Now that threshold,
> The water of the eye where the world walks
> Delicately, is as a needle threaded
> From the reel of a raveling stream, to stitch
> Dissolving figures in a watered cloth,
> A damask either-sided as the shroud
> Of the lord of Ithaca, labored at in light,
> Destroyed in darkness, while the spidery oars
> Carry his keel across deep mysteries
> To harbor in unfathomable mercies.

The poet is punning on "threshold" and it is a felicitous choice, because "thresh" has many connections throughout the sequence: that of seed, of harvest, and again, the "husk of a heart"; "hold" would have the obvious one of "hole," echoing "the pit where zero's eye is closed," and that place where white water may "fall and fall." The threshold is described in terms of a meniscus, that fragile concavity-convexity of capillarity which disappears when anything attempts to penetrate it, which causes any "strider" who walks on the water to drown. Or, the threshold is like the "tense, curved membrane" of a camera lens, "the battering light" on the side of life and movement, and darkness on the other

19. The figure of Cain is the object of a full development in the poetic drama *Cain* by Nemerov.

side. The price of crossing that membrane is to become fixed in time and space. Again, the threshold is compared to a needle threaded with a "raveling stream" which sews a cloth whose figures constantly dissolve—the fabric of life. There is a sexual level to the language throughout most of this rune: "threshold," "curved membrane," "the battering light." The membrane is crossed and figures are stitched or created in the watery cloth of life. And almost bringing us to full circle is the reappearance of Ulysses, "the lord of Ithaca." Penelope sews by day and unravels by night to save her lord, because once the sewing is finished, her lord is given up for dead and it becomes his shroud. All the while she is sewing, the "spidery oars" (spidery because spiders can walk on the surface of water) carry the sailor across mysteries such as have been pondered in these stanzas, to a harbor of mercies that cannot be measured or known.

The concluding stanza completes, in every sense of that word, the fifteen-poem sequence.

> To watch water, to watch running water
> Is to know a secret, seeing the twisted rope
> Of runnels on the hillside, the small freshets
> Leaping and limping down the tilted field
> In April's light, the green, grave and opaque
> Swirl in the millpond where the current slides
> To be combed and carded silver at the fall;
> It is a secret. Or it is not to know
> The secret, but to have it in your keeping,
> A locked box, Bluebeard's room, the deathless thing
> Which it is death to open. Knowing the secret,
> Keeping the secret—herringbones of light
> Ebbing on beaches, the huge artillery
> Of tides—it is not knowing, it is not keeping,
> But being the secret hidden from yourself.

Now that the secret has been unfolded in the sequence, we know that to watch "running water" is also to know that in one sense it is running away. This is to know a secret. And with this vision, elements in nature take on a complexity: the runnels become "the twisted rope" with connotations of death and hanging. "The small freshets" leap, but they also limp down the hillside, or "tilted field." The green of the hillside is "grave" or solemn, but it also connotes the grave, the "opaque," or that which is impervious to the light, as well as the obscure or mysterious. The water is "combed and carded silver at the fall" as it goes over the sluice. "At the fall" has obvious multiple meanings; "combed and carded silver" is richly meaningful in terms of the whole sequence. The long stalks of the sunflower in Rune III were "raking [combing] out of true" to finally crack; the rushing water turns silver, calling up obvious associations with age. And silver also recalls, from the same Rune III, the "tarnished silver" of the spent and fallen sunflower seeds.

Nemerov has written elsewhere that water can convey for him the dialectic of reality, and maybe this last rune is an obvious example of the way it can function for him. Running water poses a mystery; and one answer is that if one knows running water, one seems to know a secret. This answer does not satisfy and so he reaches another one which is—"not to know / The secret, but to have it in your keeping." To have what in your keeping? The "deathless thing." Perhaps this is what the stillness in moving things, or running water, says to him: he has the "deathless thing," being, in him like a locked box, and to know in its totality the "deathless thing" would be to die. The language of falling away and destruction continues, the light ebbing, the running water of the tides compared to artillery.

From this thesis-antithesis meditation comes his synthesis: "being the secret hidden from yourself." Recall again the words of Heidegger. "The essential relation between death and language flashes up before us, but remains still unthought. It can, however, beckon us toward the way in which the nature of language draws us into its concern and so relates us to itself, in case death belongs together with what reaches out for us, touches us. . . ." Note especially, "in case death belongs together with what reaches out for us." The stillness in moving things is not merely death, not the futile dead end of the middle of the sequence, although it may "belong together" with what reaches out for us, but rather it is the soundless gathering call . . . the ringing of stillness. It is the language of being.

"Runes," it seems to me, is one of the most artful compositions of its kind in contemporary poetry, and it is Nemerov at his best. It is perhaps a cliché to raise the ghost of Bach when speaking of such a rich, polyphonic form, but it is this kind of invention, of resonance and development, that the sequence resembles. Speaking more broadly, the poems discussed in this chapter evince a world that is as paradoxical as time itself—time which gives continuity to life, but which brings death—a world that brings the running stream with its beauty and despair, but also the stillness of being.

3

Language, Mirrors, and the Art

The complete entity, or "integer" as Nemerov calls poetry in "Lion and Honeycomb," is a result of the tension among perception, things, and words. The certainty about the relationship varies with the individual poem. In this chapter I should like first to examine the poems that take up this relationship. Observing that Nemerov often refers to language as a mirror, I should like to examine this most persistent metaphor and explain why it is integral to his vision. Then I would like to consider his attitudes about what constitutes good poetry, about the value of the imaginative life, and finally, about the source of good poetry.

Language

How is it that language speaks? How is language related to thought and thing? The poet has engaged these matters in all their complexity, and it is the nature of the engagement that singles out Nemerov among his contemporaries, an engagement characterized not only by his attentiveness to the mysterious relationship among thought, word, and thing, but also by his "listening" to other thinkers thinking about the relationship. He has remarked in an essay entitled "Attentiveness and Obedience" that "I do not now, if I ever did, consent to the common modern view of language as a system of conventional signs for the passive reception of experience, but tend ever more to see language as making an unknowably large part of a material world whose independent existence might be likened to that of the human unconscious, a sleep of causes, a chaos of the possible-impossible, responsive only to the wakening touch of desire and fear—that is, to spirit; that is, to the word."[1] This is about as clear a statement as one could seek concerning a matter that is at best mysterious. The material world (a sleep of causes) may be awakened and become responsive to the word. Clearly *word* is being used in a special sense. It is to be distinguished from just any sign that can be written or spoken. Mere conventional signs may not awaken and let show the "sleep of causes." The distinction is very like the one made in Heidegger's "The Way to Language."

> But then, in this short account of the nature of language, in what way are we thinking of speech and what is spoken? They reveal themselves even now as that by which and within which something is given voice and language, that is, makes an appearance *insofar as something is said.* To say and to speak are not identical. A man may speak, speak endlessly, and all the time say nothing. Another may remain silent, not speak at all and yet, without speaking, say a great deal.
>
> But what does "say" mean? In order to find out, we must stay close to what our very language tells us to think when we use the word. "Say" means to show, to let appear, to let be seen and heard.[2]

Heidegger writes elsewhere (in the essay "The Nature of Language") about what our very language tells us. There he informs us that *to say* is related to the Old Norse word meaning *to show* (see the passage quoted in the introduction), "to offer and extend what we call World, lighting and

1. Nemerov, *Reflexions on Poetry and Poetics,* 165–66.
2. Heidegger, *On the Way to Language,* 122.

concealing it."[3] Nemerov refers to a similar distinction in "Attentiveness and Obedience" (*RPP*). "To see certain simplicities and to say over the certain simplicities—they are in a sense the same thing; a philosopher of language tells us that see and say come from the same root, 'for to "say" is to make someone else "see" vicariously that which you have "seen." ' "[4]

Thus authentic words or "saying" reveal the "sleep of causes." The poem that bears most directly on this is "Firelight in Sunlight" (*BS*). Here the poet sees deeply into a mystery as "apple logs unlock their sunlight." He responds to this moment ecstatically. "These are my mysteries to see / And say and celebrate with words / In orders until now reserved." There are limitations to what the poet will do with this experience: he will "see" and "say," he will "celebrate." He does not say he will explain the mystery. The concluding passage of the poem tells just what magical power language possesses.

> For light is in the language now,
> Carbon and sullen diamond break
> Out of the glossary of earth
> In holy signs and scintillations,
> Release their fiery emblems to
> Renewal's room and morning's room
> Where sun and fire once again
> Phase in the figure of the dance
> From far beginnings here returned,
> Leapt from the maze at the forest's heart,
> O moment where the lost is found.

The poet here is "finding again the world," as he wrote about in "The Blue Swallows," (or is going "back to the things themselves," in the way of phenomenologists). He listens

---

3. *Ibid.*, 93.
4. Nemerov, *Reflexions on Poetry and Poetics,* 167.

attentively to the "far beginnings," "the maze at the forest's heart." He "hears" the ringing stillness of being.

While poets and thinkers have a special relationship with language, Nemerov does not treat language as their exclusive property. He knows that it is the gift of all, as he says in "To Lu Chi" (*MW*).

> The alphabet, the gift of god
> Or of the gods (and modern as we are,
> We have no better theory yet), was not
> Devised to one use only, but to all
> The work that human wit could find for it;
> Is honorably employed in government
> And all techniques; without it, nothing.

But he is irritated by the use the "active man" and the politician put to language and who in turn disparage the poet's use of language. What is the remedy for this?

> . . .Nothing but this, old sir: *continue.*
> And to the active man, if he should ask
> (If he should bother asking) Why? say nothing.
> And to the thinker, if he should ask us once
> Instead of telling us, again say nothing,
> But look into the clear and mirroring stream
> Where images remain although the water
> Passes away. Neither action nor thought,
> Only the concentration of our speech
> In fineness and in strength (your axe again),
> Till it can carry, in those other minds,
> A nobler action and a purer thought.

The poet, because he believes that in fact he has some sense of essential reality to convey to the "active man," should continue to create an effective vehicle that can carry the nobler action and the purer thought of this reality.

Some of the qualities of this vehicle, words and metaphors, are suggested in the first half of the poem, "One Way" (*BS*).

> The way a word does when
> It senses on one side
> A thing and on the other
> A thought; at either side
> It glances and goes deep
> Together; like sunlight
> On marble, on burnished wood,
> That seems to be coming from
> Within the surface and
> To be one substance with it—

The complex and mysterious character of the word (and metaphor) reflects the forces that feed in to make up its composition. The sunlight illuminates the marble or the burnished wood, and in turn, it is the nature of these objects to radiate, adding to the illumination: "That seems to be coming from / Within the surface and / To be one substance with it." The radiation of these beautiful objects is "seen" because the imagination has opened itself to being, and "seen" because of the *immediate* presence of the subject. The poem goes on to suggest a parallel in being and language.

> That is one way of doing
> One's being in a world
> Whose being is both thought
> And thing, where neither thing
> Nor thought will do alone
> Till either answers other;
> Two lovers in the night
> Each sighing other's name
> Whose alien syllables
> Become synonymous
> For all their mortal night

And their embodied day:
  Fire in the diamond
  Diamond in the dark.

One's being becomes authentic as thought and thing "become synonymous." One becomes "Saying," becomes the word as one realizes his being.

The confidence embodied in these poems is mitigated in others. One aspect of this problem involves the very distortion of reality that words and style may create. In a poem entitled "Style" (*BS*) the speaker thanks Flaubert for two novels that he did not write. In the final lines he explains his gratitude.

              They can be read,
      With difficulty, in the spirit alone,
      Are not so wholly lost as certain works
      Burned at Alexandria, flooded at Florence
      And are never taught at universities.
      Moreover, they are not deformed by style,
      That fire that eats what it illuminates.

Style, that peculiarly individual manifestation of language, appears to relate thought to thing within some kind of indeterminacy principle. The very act of measuring distorts that which is being measured, deforms, and "eats what it illuminates." After a fashion, Heidegger says something similar in numerous places.

    Poetry's spoken words shelter the poetic
    statement as that which by its essential nature
    remains unspoken. . . .

    But when does language speak itself as lan-
    guage? Curiously enough, when we cannot
    find the right word for something that con-

cerns us, carries us away, oppresses or encour-
ages us. Then we leave unspoken what we
have in mind and, without rightly giving it
thought, undergo moments in which language
itself has distantly and fleetingly touched us
with its essential being. . . .

. . .the relation of word to thing, more precisely: the mysteriousness of that relation,
which reveals itself as mystery at just that
point where the poet wants to name a prize
which he holds plainly in his hand.[5]

Thus for Heidegger and Nemerov there is a paradox involved
in trying to "say." The more one tries to "say" the truth
about essential being, the more one discovers just at that
point the mysteriousness of the relationship.

At points Nemerov may seem to drift away from "intentionality," away from "the things themselves," to the position that reality, as far as man can know it, is a symbolic
construction, and that further, the language-makers respond
in individual, reality-creating patterns. In the poem "Writing"
(*MW*) he says that words "Being intelligible / . . . become /
miraculous, so intimately, out there / at the pen's point or
brush's tip, do world / and spirit wed," but then he adds
that "The universe induces / a different tremor in every
hand." If the poem stopped here, we would be left perhaps
with a kind of psychologism; however, the poem ends insisting on a faith in the world of things.

Miraculous. It is as though the world
were a great writing. Having said so much,
let us allow there is more to the world
than writing; continental faults are not
bare convoluted fissures in the brain.
Not only must the skaters soon go home;

5. Heidegger, 188, 59, 79.

also the hard inscription of their skates
is scored across the open water, which long
remembers nothing, neither wind nor wake.

But like most experiences of faith, there are points at which
the faith is challenged.

This challenge is evident in "In the Black Museum"
(*BS*). The poem seems to reflect an attempt by the self to
disengage from its own subjectivity and when it does, "When
all analogies are broken / The scene grows strange again. At
last / There is only one of everything." Metaphor, a form of
analogy, is abrogated and the objects stand alone, like (to use
analogy) "bearded herms," "blunt instruments." Perhaps
"one mask / To every skull," which is the end of art, means
that art is a kind of congruent symbolic construct of reality.
This is the "hard, two-headed saying." This view of perception and of art concedes nothing to a metaphysics, the
speaker insists.

Nemerov sometimes becomes ironic about the symbolic
representation of art, for if the mind reflects reality through
symbol, reality may well be a reflection of mind. This has a
futility about it, "As in my dream one night a sliding
door / Opened upon another sliding door." In addition, the
poem concludes with one of Nemerov's ubiquitous mirror
images which suggests that language and art as avenues to
truth may only result in a dead-end game:

Or as two mirrors vacuum-locked together
Exclude, along with all the world,
A light to see it by. Reflect on that.

Now the reader understands why the museum is black. The cir-
cularity of man's attempt to know, as it is suggested in the
poem, reminds one of the story about the man who rang
the hour with church bells and who got the correct time by
telephoning the woman who ran the time service, who set her
watch by the ringing church bells. In addition, Nemerov's

choice of a museum to convey the idea of the poem may suggest that perception is always reflecting the past, for one cannot perceive what has not yet happened.

Mirrors

As one moves about in the poetic world of Howard Nemerov, the poet's frequent use of mirrors as metaphors becomes more and more apparent. It is the mirror that he so often uses as a vehicle for his thoughts concerning the world outside the knowing subject. There is not a single valence, however, for the mirrors, though their functions relate to one another. He has remarked in a passage from "Attentiveness and Obedience" that water in its many forms, which includes of course a reflecting pool, is a most appropriate "emblem for human life and the life of the imagination."[6] In another essay from *Reflexions on Poetry and Poetics* (1972), "The Difficulty of Difficult Poetry," Nemerov fashions his own version of the Narcissus story, saying that he "should like to redeem Narcissus from the contempt heaped on his pretty head by psychoanalysts."

When I looked into the still pool, and saw my image, I was not deluded into believing it was the image of another. I knew myself, you see, and on that account, as Tiresias said, I was doomed to die young. Let me remind you how it is when one looks into the still pool.

First, there is the water, already hard to describe except for what you see in it, just as it is hard to say what time is except by saying what happens in it. All the same, just as with time you know it is there, a medium in which something happens. You see the water, you see into the water, you see things in the water and things reflected on its surface, all at once

6. Nemerov, *Reflexions on Poetry and Poetics,* 172.

and indistinguishably. . . . And in, of, on, rove
through all this shimmering spectacle you see
your own face, your eyes are searching into
your own eyes, which hold also the sky, the
water-floor, the doubled tree, and the tension
of the surface itself. A fish or a frog swims by,
a strider dimples the film of the surface, a
drop of water falls from a leaf above, or a
breeze arises. The image is troubled, it wavers,
vanishes, reappears.

What I seemed to see, what seemed to me
to demand such profound, long and loving
regard, was this: that mortal men lived in the
world as they were reflected in the pool, their
fleeting images rove through the stuff and
fabric of the creation by whose means alone
they might define themselves; likewise, then,
a breath of air could destroy instantly this
beautiful and living tension. Studying the
pool, one's own image not more nor less essential than the simultaneous imagery of tree
and sun and star of water-floor and water
itself, seemed to me a figure for what poets
tried to do; and poetry in turn a figure for the
contemplation of truth.

So, if I may draw the moral which I consider to be appropriate, I gazed at the double
and ungraspable image of myself in the world
until I died of it; which is what all men do.
And after death I sprung up again as flower;
which again, allowing for the poetical orna-
ment—it might have been as grass—is what all
men do.[7]

There is a great deal here that helps in the understanding of
the poetry and in addition draws together in a kind of picture
the poet's position concerning reality, a way of knowing it,

7. *Ibid.*, 30–31.

and particularly the role of poetry in relation to these things. As the reader searches the body of Nemerov's work, so often he finds that the mirror the poet uses or refers to is the mirror of a reflecting water surface. This is not altogether different from silvered glass (which of course he uses, too), but the difference is important. Reflecting water corresponds more closely to the poet's conception of reality as flux and rhythm. The appropriateness of this kind of mirror is evidenced in poems already examined: "Sanctuary," "Angel and Stone," "This, That, and the Other," "Breaking of Rainbows," and certain of the "Runes." The mirror reflexions found in nature serve as analogies; language, and particularly poetry, serves as a "means of contemplation"—contemplation of reality. Part of reality, of course, is the self, and it too is included in the poem.

Thus, the mirror of "Holding the Mirror Up to Nature" is poetry. It is a very special mirror. It is the product of civilization and it can generate civilization, indeed is crucial to its maintenance.

> Some shapes cannot be seen in a glass,
> those are the ones the heart breaks at.

And these shapes are much of what poetry concerns itself with: matters of the human heart. Through the magic of this mirror, these shapes can be known—shapes that result because of relationships nurtured in the garden of civilization. It is interesting to consider what Nemerov has written in this regard.

> Language, then, is the marvelous mirror of the human condition, a mirror so miraculous that it can see what is invisible, that is, the relations between things. At the same time, the mirror is a limit, and as such, it is sorrowful; one wants to break it and look beyond. But unless we have the singular talent for mystical

experience we do not really break the mirror, and even the mystic's experience is available to us only as reflected, inadequately, in the mirror. Most often man deals with reality by its reflection. That is the sense of Perseus' victory over the Gorgon by consenting to see her only in the mirror of his shield, and it is the sense of the saying in Corinthians that we see now as through a glass darkly—a phrase rendered by modern translators as "now we see as in a little mirror."

Civilization, mirrored in language, is the garden where relations grow; outside the garden is the wild abyss.[8]

The mention of the mystical attempt to "break the mirror" and to go beyond language is part of the subject matter of "The Sanctuary," a poem examined in Chapter I. In that poem perception seemed for a moment to break through the "mirror" of the trout stream, and mind and matter took on an unusual relationship. As Nemerov notes in the essay, however, this experience is only available to others through language.

At least for the present, it appears that man can most adequately understand and describe reality, with its beautiful and horrible aspects, in terms of various symbologies such as language and mathematics. Using such "mirrors," Nemerov notes, was the only effective way Perseus could see Medusa and survive. In "A Predecessor of Perseus" (*NRD*), the poet has treated this subject from the point of view of someone who has not yet understood this.

> Since he is older than Hamlet or Stavrogin,
> Older than Leopold Bloom; since he has been
> Stravaging through the Dark Wood several years
> Beyond the appointed time, meeting no wolf,

8. Nemerov, *Poetry and Fiction: Essays,* 11–12.

Leopard, or lion, not to mention Virgil;
And long since seen the span of Keats conclude,
And the span of Alexander,—he begins
At last to wonder.

Had his sacred books
Misled him? Or had he deceived himself?
Like some he knew, who'd foolishly confused
The being called and being chosen; they
Ran down the crazy pavement of their path
On primrose all the way.

An old friend said,
"The first thing to learn about wisdom is
This, that you can't do anything with it."
Wisdom. If that was what he had, he might,
Like a retired witch, keep it locked up
In the broom closet. But he rides his road,
Passing the skinless elder skeletons
Who smile, and maybe he will keep on going
Until the grey unbearable she of the world
Shall raise her eyes, and recognize, and grin
At her eternal amateur's approach,
All guts no glass, to meet her gaze head on
And be stricken in the likeness of himself
At least, if not of Keats or Alexander.

This solitary figure is older than Shakespeare's Hamlet, Dos-
toyevsky's Stavrogin, Joyce's Bloom, and Dante's Dante,
creations or mirrors that the creators made to understand
reality—mirrors that now help us to face the Gorgon. He is
solitary and he now begins to doubt if he has been called to
this task of facing the Gorgon. But he accepts the challenge,
knowing that others have failed: "Passing the skinless elder
skeletons / Who smile." Maybe he will fail; all the others
have. But, the voice in the poem observes, the amateur has
guts if he has no glass, and even if he does not overcome
Medusa, there will remain the permanence of the likeness of
himself. Thus, this parable of the poet-seer and his lifelong

pursuit of reality is particularly the parable of the modern artist.

The world reflected in "Dead River" (*BS*) points to the limits of what can be known by the limits of the mirror.

> Passive and dark, dead river,
> Drifting beneath the images
> Received in one sole moving eye,
> Beginning nowhere, never
> Arriving, ever to be done;
> Reflecting back in black
> The leaves, the sky, the silver sun,
> Dead river, you still give
> Your still moving negative
> Down to the still glade
> Where the beaver has made
> His sill of speckled mud
> And saplings silver-dry,
> Deliverance of the sun,
> Dead river, past which never,
> Dead river, beyond which not,
>
> While summer dries away in gold
> Jeweled with bright and buzzing flies.

Thus, the mirror in Nemerov's poetry is a variable image. In this case it is dark and dead. Even though the river has been dammed by beavers there is still a slightly perceptible drift beneath the images. The river seems to have no source, it never gets where it is going entirely, and its movement is never finished. This could be said about human perception or human knowledge. Yet there are limits: "Dead river, past which never, / Dead river, beyond which not." The world wheels above, and whatever comes into view is imaged there, but nothing beyond the limits of the banks.

Concurrent with the reflection of the "dead" river is a summer that is dying and "dries away in gold." And although the anagoge of these signs is always death, the poem ends in a mystery that, paradoxically, is not entirely black, though death permeates the experience. The summer is "jeweled with bright and buzzing flies." This recalls, after a fashion, Richard Eberhart's "The Groundhog," where the speaker is walking in the golden fields of summer and comes upon a dead groundhog. As he looks at this he observes:

> There lowly in the vigorous summer
> His form began its senseless change,
> And made my senses waver dim
> Seeing nature ferocious in him.
> Inspecting close his maggots' might
> And seething cauldron of his being,
> Half with loathing, half with a strange love,
> I poked him with an angry stick.
> The fever arose, became a flame
> And vigor circumscribed the skies,
> Immense energy in the sun,
> And through my frame a sunless trembling.

For Nemerov, just as for Eberhart, there is a haunting mystery in the fact that death can dry "away in gold." Perhaps, too, there is an aesthetic assertion here that is similar to that found in Stevens' "Sunday Morning" where he writes: "Death is the mother of beauty."

Mirror imagery appears in at least twenty-five poems in a very direct way and, indirectly, in numerous others; therefore, it is not possible here to examine all such examples. Perhaps "The View" (*BS*) might serve as a final selection, and the Narcissus stance of the *persona* is likewise in evidence.

> Under his view the wind
> Blows shadows back and forth
> Across the lawn beneath
> The blowing leaves. And now
> Into his silent room
> Noon whistles, or a cry

Comes from the road where to
Is fro. Inquietude!
He walks from room to room,
From empty room to room
With the white curtains blowing.
He goes down to the kitchen
And takes from the cold tap
A glass of water pale
As glass. In the long hall
He stares into the mirror
And wills that it should break
Under his image, but
It does not break. Once more
He comes to stand before
The window and the screen,
Framing as in a graph
The view he has of flowers,
Of fields beyond the flowers,
The hanging hill, the blue
Distance that voids his vision
Though not as tears might do.
He has no tears, but knows
No one will come, there's no
Comfort, not the least
Saving discrepancy
In a view where every last thing
Is rimed with its own shadow
Exactly, and every fall
    Is once for all.

There is again the solitariness that most often accompanies the speaker in Nemerov's poetry. In addition, the monotony is largely undelineated: "Noon whistles, or a cry / Comes from the road where to / Is fro." With nothing else to do, the speaker walks aimlessly about the house, drinks a glass of water, and then stares at the mirror. Somehow he would like to break out of himself, or more likely, he wishes that his perception could go beyond the limits (as in "The Sanctuary" and others). But the mirror will not break. As the poem draws to a close, the speaker stoically accepts the hopelessness of his plight, but there is no comfort. Somehow if there was a single thing that was not "rimed with its own shadow" there would be hope. Maybe the kind of hope that might spring from knowledge that transcends "normal" human experience.

The Art

What constitutes the good poem for Nemerov? Perhaps a good place to begin is his introduction to Miller Williams' book *A Circle of Stone.*

> It may also be said that poems demanding ingenuity are bad, or "out," or whatever. To which I can say only that I prefer poems which want to be read hard and which respond to the closest attention . . . it is a matter rather of how you approach one thought through another with an effect of surprise; a matter of the steepness of the gradient between the immediate and the inferred.[9]

Nemerov writes the kind of poetry that he admires in others: poems that demand ingenuity, that want to be read hard and that respond to close attention. Sometimes a single reader may feel that certain of the poems demand more ingenuity than he possesses, but there comes the conviction that eventually the hard meaning of the poems is accessible.

However, there is a paradox involved in Nemerov's practice. In several poems he seems to argue for a simplicity, as in "On Certain Wits" (*NSP*),

9. Miller Williams, *A Circle of Stone,* with an introduction by Howard Nemerov (Baton Rouge: Louisiana State University Press, 1964), ix.

> *who amused themselves over the simplicity*
> *of Barnett Newman's paintings shown at*
> *Bennington College in May of 1958*
>
> When Moses in Horeb struck the rock,
> And water came forth out of the rock,
> Some of the people were annoyed with Moses
> And said he should have used a fancier stick.
> And when Elijah on Mount Carmel brought the rain,
> Where the prophets of Baal could not bring rain,
> Some of the people said that the rituals of
>   the prophets of Baal
> Were aesthetically significant, while Elijah's
>   were very plain.

One could argue that it is simplicity in form that Nemerov is espousing and if the experience itself is a complex one, he cannot avoid a complex poetic idea.

The old painting masters manifest the quality of simplicity that he admires (the same quality he admires in the makers of "word pictures"). In "Vermeer" (*NRD*), Nemerov says:

> Taking what is, and seeing it as it is,
> Pretending to no heroic stances or gestures,
> Keeping it simple; being in love with light
> And the marvelous things that light is able to do,
> How beautiful! a modesty which is
> Seductive extremely, the care for daily things.
>
> . . . .
>
> If I could say to you, and make it stick,
> A girl in a red hat, a woman in blue
> Reading a letter, a lady weighing gold . . .
> If I could say this to you so you saw,
> And knew, and agreed that this was how it was
> In a lost city across the sea of years,

> I think we should be for one moment happy
> In the great reckoning of those little rooms
> Where the weight of life has been lifted and
>   made light. . . .

Throughout Nemerov's own poetry, it can truly be said that he "pretends to no heroic stance." As one critic has noted, Nemerov writes about history from the point of view of the losers.[10]

In "To the Bleeding Hearts Association of American Novelists" (*NRD*), he ridicules writers who

> . . . slop their ketchup in the statue's wounds
> And advertise that blood as from the heart.
>
> I like those masters better who expound
> More inwardly the nature of our loss,
> And only offhand let us know they've found
> No better composition than a cross.

The satirical poem "On the Threshold of His Greatness, the Poet Comes Down with a Sore Throat" (*NRD*) is a *tour de force* that in its own comic, ironic way affirms simple, subtle technique, rather than the complicated. The poem is an obvious satire on some of Eliot's poetry and notes. Nemerov's poem is outweighed by the notes and as the final note ends, "poet and critic have agreed that these Notes will not merely adorn the Poem, but possibly supersede it altogether."

In a poem like "Lion & Honeycomb" (*NRD*), though, there is an insistent, candid statement about simplicity, and about an art that can endure perhaps because of its sim-

---

10. Julia Randall, "Genius of the Shore: The Poetry of Howard Nemerov," quoting Stanley Hyman, *The Hollins Critic*, Vol. VI, No. 3 (June, 1969), reprinted in Bowie Duncan (ed.), *The Critical Reception of Howard Nemerov*, 15.

plicity. This is one of Nemerov's most successful poems and
evidence of an older poet, one whose considerations are not
now of technique, but of intuitive execution. The title comes
from Judges 14, where Samson composes his riddle: "Out of
the eater came something to eat; / out of the strong came
something sweet." Perhaps one suggestion of the allusion is a
recurring one for the poet: the curiosity of creating something beautiful or useful from something of an opposing
nature. Maybe another has to do with Samsom himself. At
the end of the first section of the poem, Samsom might well
have been asking himself, "what did he want?"

> He didn't want to do it with skill,
> He'd had enough of skill. If he never saw
> Another villanelle, it would be too soon;
> And the same went for sonnets. If it had been
> Hard work learning to rime, it would be much
> Harder learning not to. The time came
> He had to ask himself, what did he want?
> What did he want when he began
> That idiot fiddling with the sounds of things?

In the second stanza the poet asks himself about the importance of technique and form.

> He asked himself, poor moron, because he had
> Nobody else to ask. The others went right on
> Talking about form, talking about myth
> And the (so help us) need for a modern idiom;
> The verseballs among them kept counting syllables.

This attitude toward an over-concern for technique is reminiscent of the remark of Gulley Jimson, that aging painter-
genius of *The Horse's Mouth.*

> Why . . . a lot of my recent stuff is not much
> better, technically, than any young lady can

do after six lessons at a good school. Heavy-
handed, stupid-looking daubery. Only difference is that it's about something—it's an experience, and all this amateur stuff is like
farting Annie Laurie through a keyhole. It
may be clever but is it worth the trouble. . . .
Sit down and ask yourself what's it all
about.[11]

Nemerov asks himself "what's it all about." He writes that
what he dreams for is "words that would / Enter the silence
and be there as a light . . . something that could stand / On
its own flat feet to keep out windy time / And the worm."

> . . . something that might simply be
> Not as the monument in the smoky rain
> Grimly endures, but that would be
> Only a moment's inviolable presence,
> The moment before disaster, before the storm,
> In its peculiar silence, an integer
> Fixed in the middle of the fall of things. . .

The integer associates itself with Samson's immortal strength
and courage as he stood in the middle of the falling temple at
Gaza.

Just as Nemerov's preferences regarding the qualities of
a good poem are clear, so is it clear that imagination takes on
its great value because it is, as he describes it, the "agent of
reality." What higher place could imagination hold? With
imagination, one can intuit even in things superficially ugly
(recall the oil and filth on the surface of the mountain stream
in "The Breaking of Rainbows" discussed in Chapter 2,
ugliness that was finally thrown off) a beauty and purity in
the stillness that lies beneath. The disparity of life lived with

11. Joyce Cary, *The Horse's Mouth* (New York: Grosset and Dunlap, 1957), 144.

and without imagination as "agent of reality" is sharp, a
disparity that is clear in the poem below from *The Salt
Garden* entitled "Truth," and not unlike what was true in
"Lion & Honeycomb."

> Around, above my bed, the pitch-dark fly
> Buzzed in the darkness till in my mind's eye
> His blue sound made the image of my thought
> An image that his resonance had brought
> Out of a common midden of the sun—
> A garbage pit, and pile where glittering tin
> Cans turned the ragged edges of their eyes
> In a mean blindness on mine . . .

The speaker, annoyed with the fly, begins to see imagina-
tively things associated with a garbage dump from somewhere
in his own past. Through what seems to be the subterranean
processes of the "secondary imagination" there is a magical
transformation.

> . . . Between dream and guess
> about a foundered world, about a wrong
> The mind refused, I waited long, long,
> And then that humming of the garbage heap
> I drew beneath the surface of my sleep
> Until I saw the helmet of the king
> Of Nineveh, pale gold and glittering
> On the king's brow, yet sleeping knew that I
> But thought the deepening blue thought of the fly.

How is the "pale gold and glittering" helmet of the king of
Nineveh related in the mind to the fly "out of a common
midden of the sun"? The Assyrians, fierce oppressors of the
Jews, collected great spoils from their conquered cities. They
were also very cruel. One Assyrian king, Ashurnisirpal, was in
the habit of cutting off the hands, feet, ears, and noses of the

captives and raising mounds of human heads. The mounds, though, the common middens, that are associated with the garbage dump of the speaker's past, likely are the mounds that are today the only remains of Nineveh. Whatever the connection, the dross of the image in the first section of the poem is transmuted into the gold of the second section through the speaker's subterranean processes.

The world of the imagination is not an escape from pain and death, valuable though such an escape might be. The relationship of death and the imagination is such that if "death belongs together with what reaches out for us"—that is, being—then our own existence becomes revitalized, transformed, becomes authentic through this agent of reality. As in "The Snow Globe" (*SG*), the associational links to the beautiful may be very somber.

> A long time ago, when I was a child,
> They left my light on while I went to sleep,
> As though they would have wanted me beguiled
> By brightness if at all; dark was too deep.
>
> And they left me one toy, a village white
> With the fresh snow and silently in glass
> Frozen forever. But if you shook it,
> The snow would rise up in the rounded space
>
> And from the limits of the universe
> Snow itself down again. O world of white,
> First home of dreams! Now that I have my dead,
> I want so cold an emblem to rehearse
> How many of them have gone from the world's light,
> As I have gone, too, from my snowy bed.

The adult is seeking his "petites madeleines" and "magic lantern" as he seeks an emblem to understand the past.

The world of "Sleeping Beauty" (*SG*) is likewise a complicated one. A child is told the fairy tale of "Sleeping Beauty." Then he dreams of kings and queens. Of course, when the princess is kissed, all the people awaken and " begin to forget / Whatever they dreamed that was so like a dream." Then the speaker asks if he should forget that he was the source of the dreaming.

> And shall I also, with the kiss, forget
> That I was the one who dreamed them all,
> Courtier and king, scullion and cook,
> Horse in the stable and fly on the wall?
> Forget the petals' whisper when they drift
> Down where the untold princes die in blood
> Because I dreamed the thicket and the thorn?

Shall he forget that he is the one who is the dreamer and is capable of making the dreams? But more difficult, shall he forget the sadness of the petals' whisper and the untold princes who die in blood? His dream is not just of princesses who wake, but of thickets and thorns.

"Sunglasses" (*MW*) presents only a qualified refuge. The sunglasses protect the speaker from the blinding light of the sun, and thus he is unpunished by the "outer world." This permits him to dream "unmolested," but his dream's pleasure is alloyed with despair.

> Against my glass, all light is pacified
> Here where I lie in green gone deeper green,
> All colors colder; I, dreaming I died
> Where in still waters on illusion's coast
> The cold-eyed sirens sang to sailor men
> Of jewels that charred the zenith, and were lost.

His self-consciousness and wit never far away, the poet ridicules the experience of one fantasizer in "The Map-Maker on His Art" (*MW*). As in the poem "To Lu Chi," the active and the contemplative man are compared, but this kind of "contemplative man" does not fare so well.

After the bronzed, heroic traveler
Returns to the television interview
And cocktails at the Ritz, I in my turn
Set forth across the clean, uncharted paper.
Smiling a little at his encounters with
Savages, bugs, and snakes, for the most part
Skipping his night thoughts, philosophic notes,
Rainy reflexions, I translate his trip
Into my native tongue of bearings, shapes,
Directions, distances.

. . . .

                    This my modest art
Brings wilderness well down into the range
Of any budget; under the haunted mountain
Where he lay in delirium, deserted
By his safari, they will build hotels
In a year or two. I make no claim that this
Much matters (they will name a hotel for him
and none for me), but lest the comparison
Make me appear a trifle colorless,
I write the running river a rich blue
And—let imagination rage!—wild green
The jungles with their tawny meadows and swamps
Where, till the day I die, I will not go.

Nemerov's attitude toward the permanence and value of the world and works of the imagination moves up and down a scale, from hope to pessimism. In "Lightning Storm on Fuji" (*MW*) he expresses the pessimistic end of the scale. The contemplative stance of the speaker is a typical one for this poet. He first offers his reflections on Hokusai's woodblock. The storm and lightning are in the foreground, and beyond Fuji rises in serenity, high above the violence below. Clearly this is art, he says, not nature.

A picture, then, touching eternity
From time, the way Fuji touches the sky,

Transparently, so that the summit might
Be substance thin enough to pierce with light.
The subject, you may say, is violence,
Or storm, and calm rising above the storm
To the region of serenity and splendor
Where earthly things are seen as a clear light.
This subject is imitated in the form.

Then the poet tells us he has been watching the woodblock
for a long while and that from time to time he looks out the
window at a small mountain in his native America, which is
named after Mad Anthony Wayne, man of action and revolu-
tionary general. The evening light fades and with it both
mountains. What follows are some memorable lines by
Nemerov:

Between eternity and time there is
Space for the terrible thought that all things fail.
I try to think it through the evening, while
Shadows emerge and merge upon the mountain
And night grows up the slow flank heaved like a wave
Out of the first fault of the ancient earth,
To hold in silence till another morning
The folded history which will dream away,
Defined or not in nature, action, art,
Mad Anthony and Hokusai and me.

The eternal value of art and the historical value of action
seem to come to nothing during this particular meditative
moment. Only the ancient earth appears to hold within itself
the power to endure.

In much the same way that the speaker examines the
woodblock does he, in "Shells" (*MW*), pick up and study the
sea shell. It, too, is a thing of beauty and form, although it is
also described as "empty and light and dry." The process of
creating the shell by the mollusk is similar to creating a work
of art by the artist.

The vital waste in composition
With the beauty of the ruined remainder.

And what of the meaning of this beautiful form? Does nature reveal herself in any fundamental way? If she does, it is very economically.

Its form is only cryptically
Instructive, if at all: it winds
Like generality, from nothing to nothing

By means of nothing but itself.

And as in "Lightning Storm on Fuji" the poem concludes with a statement concerning the permanence of history and art.

It is a stairway going nowhere,
Our precious emblem of the steep ascent,

Perhaps, beginning at a point
And opening to infinity,
Or the other way, if you want it the other way.

Inside it, also, there is nothing
Except the obedient sound of waters
Beat by your Mediterranean, classic heart

In bloody tides as long as breath,
Bringing by turns the ebb and flood
Upon the ruining house of histories,

Whose whitening stones, in Africa,
Bake dry and blow away, in Athens,
In Rome, abstract and instructive as chalk

When children scrawl the blackboard full
Of wild spirals every which way,
To be erased with chalk dust, then with water.

It becomes clear, however, that although Nemerov may
sometimes be skeptical about the permanence of art, his
work reveals a faith in the revelatory character of art, especially art as a vehicle of insight into the deep and beautiful
processes of the natural world. Many of the poems that we
have looked at in this chapter are evidence of this. While
"Lightning Storm on Fuji" closes on a skeptical note concerning permanence, Hokusai's conception and execution of
his vision of Fuji offer a two-fold revelation at least: one part
concerning Fuji as an object itself, and the second concerning
the nature of reality in a larger sense. In "Lion & Honeycomb" the speaker declares that what he wants is "words
that would / Enter the silence and be there as a light." This
is part of what Nemerov admires about the master's art in
"Vermeer": it can, by "taking what is, and seeing it as it is"
lift the weight of life and make it light (and I take his "light"
in both senses). In the last four lines of "The Blue Swallows,"
there is a testament to the powers of the imagination.

Finding again the world,
That is the point, where loveliness
Adorns intelligible things
Because the mind's eye lit the sun.

Finally, in "The Winter's Lightning" (SG) there is a
lucid statement concerning art as revelation.

Over the snow at night,
And while the snow still fell,
A sky torn to the bone
Shattered the ghostly world with light;

As though this were the moon's hell,
A world hard as a stone,
  Cold, and blue-white.

As if the storming sea
Should sunder to its floor,
And all things hidden there
Gleam in the moment silently,
So does the meadow at the door
To split and sudden air
  Show stone and tree.

From the drowned world of dark
The sleeping innocence
Surrenders all its seeming;
Under the high, charged carbon arc
Light of the world, a guilty sense
Stiffens the secret dreaming
  Animal park.

So in the camera's glare
The fortunate and famed,
For all their crooked smiles,
Reveal through their regarded stare
How all that's publicly acclaimed
One brutal flash reviles
  For cold despair.

So is the murderer caught
When his lost victim rises
Glaring through dream and light
With icy eyes. That which was thought
In secret, and after wore disguises,
Silts up the drowning sight
  Mind inwrought.

So may the poem dispart
The mirror from the light
Where none can see a seam;

The poet, from his wintry heart
And in the lightning second's sight,
Illuminate this dream
    With a cold art.

At this point an interesting comparison might be made to certain poems of Wallace Stevens. In an article "Wallace Stevens and the State of Winter Simplicity," George Lensing has singled out (among other poems) "The Snow Man," "An Ordinary Evening in New Haven," and "No Possum, No Sop, No Taters." He says about such poems that "winter represents that dimension of reality totally devoid of subjective imposition: the setting is 'crusted with snow' and 'the same bare place.' The 'mind of winter' is a psychic state toward which all subjective consciousness moves, in order to attain that position of identity with reality."[12]   There may be a question as to whether "winter" and "cold" in this context would have an identical meaning in the poem "The Winter's Lightning." But, Lensing says that winter for Stevens would be a non-subjective vision and it might well be argued that this is the case in the poem by Nemerov. The poet asks for an art that will cause "all things hidden" to be revealed. And particularly he asks for an art that can reveal the difference in the genuine source of light and its reflection.

To summarize this section, the imagination as "agent of reality" seems to take on the character of a universe as organism which moves in a purposeful direction, which loses nothing that can be saved, in that imagination may take the dross and ugliness of the world and transmute it. This idea was intrinsic to many of the poems discussed in this section. Further, there was additional evidence of the power of the imagination to reveal "the sleep of causes," to act as an agent of reality, or put another way, to have the power to sign reality's name.

12. George Lensing, "Wallace Stevens and the State of Winter Simplicity," *Southern Review,* New Series, VII, No. 3 (July, 1971), 767.

There remains to consider what might be called the sources of great poetry. In "Maestria" (*NSP*) Nemerov explores the anomalies that seem to co-exist with mastery.

MAESTRIA

Is where you find it,
And you need not agree with its views
About money or the meaning of numbers,
About the immaculate conception or the divine
Ancestry of Augustus.

. . . .

                                            Doubtless
It would be better to be always right, refraining
From those millennial expectations, but strangely,
Rising sometimes from hatred and wrong,
The song sings itself out to the end,
And like a running stream which purifies itself
It leaves behind the mortality of its maker,
Who has the skill of his art, and a trembling hand.

It is apparent that the attitude here is an undirected rebuttal to Ruskin's thesis in *The Stones of Venice* that the rise or fall of Venetian Gothic art depends on the moral or immoral temper of the state. Obviously Nemerov did not initiate the objections and questions that "Maestria" raises. In the closing chapter of *A Portrait of the Artist as a Young Man* Stephen Daedalus poses one of his famous questions that is related to the ideas in Nemerov's poem. " 'If a man hacking in fury at a block of wood,' . . . 'make there an image of a cow, is that image a work of art? If not, why not?' "[13] Whether a man is a Fascist or a Catholic, his poetry stands beyond ideology and contemporary politics insofar as he truly possesses

13. James Joyce, *A Portrait of the Artist as a Young Man* (New York: The Viking Press, 1960), 214.

"maestria." After the smoke has "blown off those battle-fields," what of Shakespeare remains is not dependent upon his being a royalist or not, an Anglican or not. Conversely, propaganda of any sort is not the essential source of art, although clearly this may seem to be the beginning to the reader and artist alike sometimes.

So the source of great poetry is "maestria." And how does a young man know if he has maestria in order that he may be encouraged to write poetry? Well, he does not. When Nemerov addressed his fellow professionals at the Library of Congress on 23 October 1962, he had this to say that bears on our question:

> ... that the poet may in fact be an inferior soul altogether is an occupational hazard. I mean only that when something comes to you to be dealt with according to such skill and energy as you may have to give it, you give it what you have; which may not be much, or nearly enough, but excludes for the time all thought of whether it will be acceptable to "the public"—an entity, I repeat, of which poets have very little opportunity of forming an image.
>
> The poet hopes to articulate a vision con-cerning human life; he hopes to articulate it truly. He may not be much of a poet, he may not be much of a human being, the vision perhaps is not so special either; but it is what he hopes to do. I stress his *hoping* to do so because much of the available evidence tells us that his effective control in the matter, his conscious will to do all this, may make no difference whatever, or none but a technical and executive difference—which I don't mean to slight, as it is not negligible, but it is not what I am talking about now .[14]

14. Nemerov, *Poetry and Fiction: Essays,* 45.

The sources of poetry? For Nemerov it is just as mysterious as it has been for so many poets. The poet is under the power of his "Muse." And attempts to be much more specific than "Muse" are at best questionable. Somehow the vast subterranean labyrinth of the poet's mind does what it seems to have to do. Note that Nemerov says, ". . .much of the available evidence tells us that his effective control in the matter, his conscious will to do all this, may make no difference whatever."

But what distinguishes Nemerov's ideas and practice concerning language, imagery, and imagination, in general, is a formulation and execution with an acute awareness of the thinking and problems of his time. There are contemporary poets who seem to have moved in a virtually direct line of descent from the early nineteenth-century Romantics, for example. Not having passed through the cold bath of scientism, of conceptions of language as "conventional signs for the passive reception of experience," such poets do not have the tempered hardness and elasticity of Nemerov.

4

Nemerov has noted that the character of his poetry changed after his second volume and that this change coincided with his move to the countryside of Vermont.[1] From this point the landscape took over his poetry—a felicitous occurrence for Nemerov's public, in my opinion, for it has been the source of his best work. As he has moved about the Vermont landscape, the poems that have come out of his experience are concrete testimony that what he finally sensed was some kind of mystery. Somehow the land "spoke" to him in an inexplicable way. After exploring the nature of this mysterious "saying" of nature, we may profitably go on to individual "sayings" or poems. What do these poems say that can be understood through language? For Nemerov, as for Heidegger, there is a paradox involved in trying to "say." The more one tries to "say" the truth about being, the more one discovers just at that point the mysteriousness of the relationship. What, however, can be conveyed?

Perhaps to illustrate an aspect of the mystery of the relationship, it will be useful to follow Nemerov in his essay "Attentiveness and Obedience." In this essay he is, in part, addressing himself to the subject of the mysterious "sayings" of nature, and he chooses the poem "A Spell before Winter" (*NRD*) to illustrate what he means:

> After the red leaf and the gold have gone
> Brought down by the wind, then by hammering rain
> Bruised and discolored, when October's flame

1. Nemerov, *Reflexions on Poetry and Poetics,* 165.

Goes blue to guttering in the cusp, this land
Sinks deeper into silence, darker into shade.
There is a knowledge in the look of things,
The old hills hunch before the north wind blows.

Now I can see certain simplicities
In the darkening rust and tarnish of the time,
And say over the certain simplicities,
The running water and the standing stone,
The yellow haze of the willow and the black
Smoke of the elm, the silver, silent light
Where suddenly, readying toward nightfall,
The sumac's candelabrum darkly flames.
And I speak to you now with the land's voice,
It is the cold, wild land that says to you
A knowledge glimmers in the sleep of things:
The old hills hunch before the north wind blows.

The speaker's attention has not been caught by the
exploding colors of a New England autumn; rather he regards
"certain simplicities / In the darkening rust" after the flam-
boyance of autumn has gone. There are several important
points to be considered here, taking the poem and Nemerov's
comments about the poem together. The figure who speaks
in the poem is much moved by a *visual* experience. Even after
the brilliant colors have gone (the reds and golds), there is the
"darkening rust and tarnish of the time," "the yellow haze of
the willow," "black / Smoke of the elm," "silver, silent
light," and the darkly flaming sumac. All of this is visual, and
the figure says "There is a knowledge in the look of things,"
"I can see certain simplicities." It is especially interesting, I
think, to read Nemerov's comment about his "aural imagination" in connection with the poem's abundant visual images.

   . . . having a dominantly aural imagination, I not so much look at nature as I listen
   to what it says. This is a mystery, at least in
   the sense that I cannot explain it—why should

a phrase come to you out of the ground and
seem to be exactly right? But the mystery
appears to me as a poet's proper relation with
things, a relation in which language, that accumulated wisdom and folly in which the
living and the dead speak simultaneously, is a
full partner and not merely a stenographer.[2]

In what way can we understand "A Spell before Winter" in
terms of an "aural imagination"; Clearly, the figure in the
poem has been *looking* at nature. It is at this point in his
essay he observes that seeing and saying over certain simplicities is in a sense the same thing, and then goes on to
quote the philosopher of language who tells us that "see and
say come from the same root, 'for to "say" is to make
someone else "see" vicariously that which you have
"seen." ' "[3]

    "Seeing" and "listening" must be taken on two levels of
discourse. The figure may see the running water or hear the
running water, and the meaning of this is what it normally is
in commonsense discourse. But the figure "sees" and "listens" to the "sleep of causes," or the "sleep of things," and
what is "heard" is the soundless gathering call, the ringing of
stillness that was discussed at the end of Chapter 2. What is
heard is the language of being. Looking again at the poem,
we notice "this land / Sinks deeper into silence." It is the
silence that "the land's voice" speaks. Clearly, then, "aural
imagination" does not mean an imagination that responds
principally to, for example, the song of a bird rather than the
sight of a bird.

    How does one relate himself properly to nature? Some
answers may be had in Nemerov's essay "The Swaying Form:
A Problem in Poetry." Mainly, he is discussing the writer's
relationship to the world, but the answers obtain more gener-
ally, I think. He calls writing a species of *askesis*, "a per-
severing devotion to the energy passing between self and

2. *Ibid.*, 166.
3. *Ibid.*, 166–67.

world. It is a way of living, a way of being. . . ."[4] In addition, one does not approach nature in the way of science, at least not some science.

> As to art's relation with science. The experimental method was defined, by Galileo, I believe, as putting nature to the question, where "the question" meant the judicial process of torture. The definition seems to imply a faith that nature, so treated, will reveal the secret name for a situation; when once that situation has been isolated, treated as a situation in itself, and considered for a moment apart from the flux of all things, nature will, as it were, confess her presumably guilty secret.
>   . . . The instruments of science, of course, have as their aim the creation of an objectivity as nearly as possible universal in character; the poet's aim might be thought of as the same and reversed, a mirror image—to represent in the world the movement of a subjectivity as nearly as possible universal in character.[5]

Rather than putting the question to nature in the way of experimental method, one listens attentively and obediently, opens oneself to being ("a swaying form") with a mediated reflexivity. Obedient, perhaps, in the way Heidegger means, describing another way of questioning: "Questioning is the piety of thinking. 'Piety' is meant here in the ancient sense: obedient, or submissive, and in this case submitting to what thinking has to think about."[6] None of this means, however, that Nemerov does not have an intense interest in the infor-

4. Nemerov, *Poetry and Fiction: Essays,* 14.
5. *Ibid.,* 15.
6. Heidegger, *On the Way to Language,* 72.

mation science has to offer, whether it be astronomy or biology.

Turning to the poem "Trees" (*MW*), we find Nemerov choosing, instead of the ubiquitous "running stream," a metaphor of organic process. The trees communicate in the way good poems do, by being and not by explaining, leaving the education to the student.

> To be a giant and keep quiet about it,
> To stay in one's own place;
> To stand for the constant presence of process
> And always to seem the same;
> To be steady as a rock and always trembling,
> Having the hard appearance of death
> With the soft, fluent nature of growth,
> One's Being deceptively armored,
> One's Becoming deceptively vulnerable;
> To be so tough, and take the light so well,
> Freely providing forbidden knowledge
> Of so many things about heaven and earth
> For which we should otherwise have no word—
> Poems or people are rarely so lovely,
> And even when they have great qualities
> They tend to tell you rather than exemplify
> What they believe themselves to be about,
> While from the moving silence of trees,
> Whether in storm or calm, in leaf and naked,
> Night or day, we draw conclusions of our own,
> Sustaining and unnoticed as our breath,
> And perilous also—though there has never been
> A critical tree—about the nature of things.

The poem mirrors the tree which mirrors the paradox of a world that seems to be "steady as a rock" but in fact is in flux, a tree which represents "the constant presence of process." The tree speaks by its silence about "which we should otherwise have no word," and this word concerns "forbidden knowledge." This revelation is "sustaining," but it is also "perilous."

Man and the things of Man are humble in the face of the awesome force that is immanent in the reality of brute substance. It is never the attitude of the scientist as Faust. As a matter of fact, Nemerov's essay "The Dream of Reason" would seek to blunt the scientist's pride and sometimes arrogance as he (in this case the geneticist) seeks to "rule" Nature. In quite a different way the poet expresses his reverence for Nature in "Human Things" (*NRD*).

When the sun gets low, in winter,
The lapstreaked side of a red barn
Can put so flat a stop to its light
You'd think everything was finished.

Each dent, fray, scratch, or splinter,
Any gray weathering where the paint
Has scaled off, is a healed scar
Grown harder with the wounds of light.

Only a tree's trembling shadow
Crosses that ruined composure; even
Nail holes look deep enough to swallow
Whatever light has left to give.

And after sundown, when the wall
Slowly surrenders its color, the rest
Remains, its high, obstinate
Hulk more shadowy than the night.

The poet's reverence for Nature might be said to take the form of a little drama. The action reflects a struggle between the man-made barn and the day and night of Nature. For three stanzas the lapstreaked side of the barn stops the light of day so that "you'd think everything was finished," and even the nail holes look deep enough to swallow the light. But in the fourth and final stanza the dramatic conflict is resolved as the wall "slowly surrenders" and becomes less substantial, even "more shadowy than the night."

"The End of Summer School" (*NRD*) speaks of a different side of the natural energy. The poet articulates what many have been moved by as the seasons change, intensifying a movement that gives meaning to our lives. In this instance it is the sudden move towards autumn. The lyric voice notes the first few leaves that detach themselves from the branches and is surprised at "How strange and slow the many apples ripened / And suddenly were red beneath the bough." While noting the end of something, he also sees seeds drifting in the wind; early in the poem he observes that the "spider's web was cold," but later he notes baby spiders who sometimes even sail on the wind far out to sea. Of nature's dialectic he writes in the closing two stanzas.

> This is the end of summer school, the change
> Behind the green wall and the steady weather:
> Something that turns upon a hidden hinge
> Brings down the dead leaf and live seed together,
>
> And of the strength that slowly warps the stars
> To strange harbors, the learned pupil knows
> How adamant the anvil, fierce the hearth
> Where imperceptible summer turns the rose.

The metaphor of summer school which began quite literally as the end of the summer school semester becomes the "summer school" where one learns of experience and the universe, and most of all, of the mysterious force that is intrinsic to the world. The pupil who studies in this school learns of the terrible and awesome force that "slowly warps the stars" and simultaneously possesses the gentlest control "Where imperceptible summer turns the rose."

Certain other poems might be said to group themselves around a feeling of joy and exaltation in the presence of wild creatures and wild landscape, just as the first group of poems emanate perhaps from a reflective awe in the presence of the natural energy. "The First Point of Aries" (*NRD*) characteristically celebrates Spring, the title referring to the first

sign of the zodiac, which the sun enters about March twenty-
first.

> After the morning of amazing rain
> (How fiercely it fell, in slanting lines of light!)
> A new breeze blew the clouds back to the hills,
> And the huge day gloried in its gold and blue.
>
> The road they walked was shoe-top deep in mud,
> But the air was mild. And water of the spring,
> The new, cold water, spread across the fields,
> The running, the wind-rippled, the still-reflecting.
>
> Life with remorseless joy possessed them then,
> Compelling happiness beyond the power
> Of prudence to refuse; perforce they gave
> To splendor their impersonal consent.
>
> What god could save them from this holy time?
> The water, blinking in the sun's blue eye,
> Watches them loiter on the road to death,
> But stricken helpless at the heart with love.

Seldom if ever is such exaltation unalloyed with an awareness
of time passing or approaching death in Nemerov's poetry,
but in this one it is not predominant. In the midst of this joy
that compels them "beyond the power / Of prudence," the
water which "watches them loiter on the road to death," is
helpless somehow, when confronted with such joy or compelled to mirror such joy—stricken because its heart fills with
love at such a sight.

Nemerov writes of spring seven years earlier in "Zal-
moxis" (SG), this time in a quieter, more meditative way.
Spring reveals itself "with a soft / Suddenness." It "soft-
ens / Coldly to life the leaves of pupal sleep." The speaker
in the poem is in his study and he responds to these beginnings by throwing open the windows, letting the stale cigar
smoke out and, "stares down the field to the wild

hill / Where on this day the sullen and powerful bear, / Drunken with deathlessness, lurches from sleep."

The knowledge of some of the "factual" workings of the natural world does not blunt the imagination of the poet but seems to enhance it. "The Dragonfly" (*NRD*) is a good example.

> Under the pond, among rocks
> Or in the bramble of the water wood,
> He is at home, and feeds the small
> Remorseless craving of his dream,
>
> His cruel delight; until in May
> The dream transforms him with itself
> And from his depths he rises out,
> An exile from the brutal night.
>
> He rises out, the aged one
> Imprisoned In the dying child,
> And spreads his wings to the new sun:
> Climbing, he withers into light.

The eggs of dragonflies are dropped in water or inserted into aquatic plants and the nymphs that are hatched remain in the water from three months to five years. After many successive molts the adult dragonfly leaves the water. There is an obvious reference to this birth struggle. He imagines the mandatory dream of the nymph who waits out his sentence under water slowly outgrowing himself. Finally spring lifts his sentence of "the brutal night" and the adult quite literally leaves the bodily prison of his younger self. There is, of course, a ruthlessness at the end of this dream of glory: as the dragonfly begins to feel his freedom, "he withers into light."

There are numerous poems like "The Dragonfly" that reflect an admiration for the courage, the mysterious will to live that establishes a kinship between all earthly creatures. Sea birds for example have often captured Nemerov's attention. One poem that celebrates this courage is "Sandpipers"

(*MW*). At first their jerky motions on the beach remind him of
funny human analogies, but then he says this comedy is
different.

> But this comedy is based upon exact
> Perceptions, and delicately balanced
> Between starvation and the sea:
> Though sometimes I have seen one slip and fall,
> From either the undertow or greed,
> And have to get up in the wave's open mouth,
> Still eating, I have never seen
> One caught; if necessary he spreads his wings,
> With white stripe, and flutters rather than flies
> Out, to begin eating again at once.
> Now they are over every outer beach,
> Procrastinating steadily southwards
> In endlessly local comings and goings.

In this comedy it is true that the sandpiper may take a fall,
but the comedy gets much closer to tragedy in the way of a
slip and fall of a Wallenda. The sandpiper is no buffoon
because he has exact perceptions and the whole action is
"delicately balanced / Between starvation and the sea."
What saves this tragedy is that the sandpiper gets up, even if
he has to flutter instead of flying, and he gets up still eating.
      But like human beings, who can seem comic one mo-
ment and glorious the next, the birds leave the poet rapt with
admiration.

> Whenever a flock of them takes flight,
> And flies with the beautiful unison
> Of banners in the wind, they are
> No longer funny. It is their courage,
> Meaningless as the word is when compared
> With their thoughtless precisions, which strikes
> Me when I watch them hidden and revealed
> Between two waves, lost in the sea's
> Lost color as they distance me; flying

From winter already, while I
Am in August. When suddenly they turn
In unison, all their bellies shine
Like mirrors flashing white with signals
I cannot read, but I wish them well.

The birds' movement first in the trough of high waves and
then as they reveal themselves suddenly in ascendancy strikes
the human observer as courageous, though he admits this is in
fact meaningless as they take flight and wheel with a precision that is not self-conscious—a prerequisite of courage.
This "admission" that their precision is "thoughtless" is
additional evidence of Nemerov's rather consistent refusal to
anthropomorphize their courage. Such a perspective is often
called non-romantic, although such ideas are more characteristic of romanticism at its worst than at its best. The
"bellies shine / Like mirrors flashing white with signals"
that the Seer cannot Interpret, but he does recognize that
they resemble some kind of sign. From what we know of the
body of Nemerov's work, these would be signs or "emblems"
of the rhythm of process and flux.
     Gulls often figure in Nemerov's nature poetry, one of
the most notable examples being found in the often antholo-
gized and often discussed poem "The Salt Garden." In that
poem and in the following poem, "The Gulls," the beauty of
the bird is explored; it is a complex beauty, a beauty com-
bined with fierceness and brutal savagery.

I know them at their worst, when by the shore
They raise the screaming practice of their peace,
Disputing fish and floating garbage or
Scraps of stale bread thrown by a child. In this,
Even, they flash with senseless beauty more
Than I believed—sweet are their bitter cries,
As their fierce eyes are sweet; in their mere greed
Is grace, as they fall splendidly to feed.

And sometimes I have seen them as they glide
Mysterious upon a morning sea

Ghostly with mist, or when they ride
White water or the shattered wind, while we
Work at a wooden oar and huddle inside
Our shallow hull against the sea-torn spray;
And there they brutally are emblems of
Soul's courage, summoners to a broken love.

Courage is always brutal, for it is
The bitter tooth fastens the soul to God
Unknowing and unwilling, but as a vise
Not to be torn away. In the great crowd,
Because it gathers from such empty skies,
Each eye is arrogant and each voice loud
With angry lust; while alone each bird must be
Dispassionate above a hollow sea.

White wanderers, sky-bearers from the wide
Rage of the waters! so may your moving wings
Defend you from the kingdom of the tide
Whose sullen sway beneath your journeyings
Wrinkles like death, so may your flying pride
Keep you in danger—bless the song that sings
Of mortal courage; bless it with your form
Compassed in calm amid the cloud-white storm.

The tension of the metaphor is not here between comedy and courage, as in "Sandpipers," but of a strange mix-
ture of ugliness, brute appetite and, again, courage. Such
a fabric, or complex, is similar to that found in poems like
"Truth" (SG) and "The Town Dump" (MW). In these poems
the juxtaposition of apparent disparities provides an unusual
kind of knowledge or awareness. "The Town Dump" is
introduced by the quotation "The art of our necessities is
strange, / That can make vile things precious." Such an
"alchemical" process likely finds its source in survival. The
poet is certainly transmuting base experience into something
beautiful. In this instance he says he knows these scavengers
"at their worst" as they fight their fellows over floating
garbage. But even in this barbarity "their mere greed / Is

grace." But there is in the poem a rising curve of admiration for these creatures. As he finds himself bound to sea level, huddled "inside / Our shallow hull" the birds become emblems of "soul's courage." The beauty of such courage is the theme of the poem and this beauty exalts the spirit of the man. In lines reminiscent of Tennyson's "The Eagle," the sea "wrinkles like death" below the gulls (which quite literally it may be if the gull is not quick). Yet the poet urges the bird's "flying pride" to keep it in danger. Without this threat, and without death, meaning in this context vanishes and certainly the meaning of a virtue like courage. The bravery creates a fortress in the midst of the hostile storm. Even though the poet has admitted in "The Sandpipers" that to talk of "courage" is meaningless when compared to the birds' "thoughtless precisions," he identifies so closely with the threat to the gulls that he speaks of their "pride."

"Deep Woods" (SG) might serve to conclude this selection of poems that represent the feeling of joy and exaltation in the presence of wild creatures and wild landscape. In "The Loon's Cry" and "Blue Swallows," among others, Nemerov speaks of living in an unsymboled world. From a different perspective the poet of "Deep Woods" has a similar experience and it is the basis for a kind of peace, or even hope. The perspective is not one in which the poet demythologizes the landscape around him but one in which mythology has not yet found roots. It is the landscape of New England woods that have never been settled or cut, virgin in many senses of the word. The poem begins, "Such places are too still for history." The poet notes that if others were to speak of these woods they would simply assume that these woods are like any other woods throughout history and throughout the world. But the poet denies this:

> This unlegended land
> Is no Black Forest where the wizard lived
> Under a bent chimney and a thatch of straw
> Nor the hot swamp theatrical with snakes
> And tigers; nor the Chinese forest on
> The mountainside, with bridge, pagoda, fog,

> Three poets in the foreground, drinking tea
> (there is no tea, and not so many as three)—
> But this land, this, unmitigated by myth
> And whose common splendors are comparable only to
> Themselves; . . .

The idea of the poem is like the idea that drew early Americans to the "New Eden" that scholars have long recognized. This is a wilderness before sin and before Cain. The "New Eden" was to be a place to leave the weary troubles and fears of the corrupt Old World. The single figure in "Deep Woods," who feels a relief in contemplating the virgin forest, is a kind of microcosmic emblem of the men who came to New England and other parts of the United States. Nemerov describes this feeling:

> But here the heart, racing strangely as though
> Ready to stop, reaches a kind of rest;
> The mind uneasily rests, as if a beast,
> Being hunted down, made tiredness and terror
> Its camouflage and fell asleep, and dreamed,
> At the terrible, smooth pace of the running dogs,
> A dream of being lost, covered with leaves
> And hidden in a death like any sleep
> So deep the bitter world must let it be
> And go bay elsewhere after better game.

The woods are not an unqualified refuge certainly. "The mind uneasily rests" and when it dreams, it dreams of being lost. Yet, "the bitter world must let it be / And go bay elsewhere after better game." Left alone the poet feels free to create his own myths: "And this is yours to work." The last portion of the poem relates various possibilities that are linked with former legends and myths. As he entertains these thoughts, the poet remarks, "More probably nothing will happen," and at the end of his considerations he concludes "Most probably / Nothing will happen." But as he con-

tinues, the reader knows the difference between the first
Adam before the Fall and this second Adam before the Fall.
He is not innocent of the past, though his woods might be.

> Even the Fall of Man
> Is waiting, here, for someone to grow apples;
> And the snake, speckled as sunlight on the rock
> In the deep woods, still sleeps with a whole head
> And has not begun to grow a manly smile.

Though the poet is not sentimentalizing the possibilities, the
deep woods are a source of peace, troubled though it might
be, and a refuge where "the bitter world must let it be."

The Anagoge Is Always Death

The omnipresence of Nemerov's sense of death as integral to natural process is soon apparent to any reader. Such
an awareness is obviously an attribute of any serious poet,
but in Nemerov's case, the awareness of death permeates
much of his work. It is significantly so with much of his
poetry that is meditative, nature poetry. The emphasis may
be on the imperturbabllIty of nature in the presence of
individual or particular ruin, as in "Midsummer's Day" (SG).
The poet is struck by "This ruinous garden an old woman
made / And fertilized with tea leaves and coffee grounds,
[which] Is wild grass mostly, climbed up to the thigh." After
a fashion, he expresses an attitude similar to "Human
Things," that the things men work at seem insignificant
compared to nature's work.

> I have looked out and seen the summer grow
> Day after day between the cracked flags
> Of the terrace where no one wishes to sit,
> And thought of fortune and family, the fine rags
> Brutal desire, poor patience, or a nice wit

Had made to be stitched together in a show
For everyone to marvel at, a pride
That must have been already withered inside.

The final stanza foretells a winter that is implicit in the hot
fecundity of summer.

Ruin remains, and nature pays no mind.
This mind, that flesh is and will go like grass
In the brief stubble burnt at harvest or
In the sun's long stare, sees as though sealed in glass
The high and silent wave over the floor
Of summer come, casting up seed and rind;
And, held upon this hill, among the trees
Hears the loud forage of the honey bees.

Mind and flesh "will go like grass" and mind sees the summer
"casting up seed and rind"; mind also hears the bees busy
working to store up honey as nature moves them toward
winter.

"The First Leaf" takes the reader further into the an-
nual cycle than "Midsummer's Day." The attentive observer
in the poem notices the first subtle change in the season as
the life goes out of summer. The following poem from *The
Salt Garden* is an example of the work Nemerov achieved
after moving to New England.

Here is one leaf already gone from green
To edged red and gold, a Byzantine
Illumination of the summer's page
Of common text, and capital presage
For chapters yet to fall. An old story,
How youth may go from glory into glory
Changing his green for a stiff robe of dry
Magnificence, taking the brilliant dye
From steeped oblivion; going, near a ghost,

Become a lord and captain of the host;
Or cardinal, in priestly full career,
Preach abstinence or at the most small beer.

Success is doubtful, you may be perplexed,
Reaching it rich, and old, and apoplexed
To bloody innocence, teaching the green
One of the things at least that life must mean,
And standing in the book of days a splen-
did summary, rubric, index of the end,
Commerced with time to great advantage, high
And singular with instruction how to die—
And immortality, though life be cheap,
For the early turncoat and the Judas sheep.

This is "an old story" the poet says he tells—how youth
becomes instead the older generation and begins to talk in
advisory or ministerial tones. And nature has something of
value to teach. It may "preach abstinence," or that "success
is doubtful." In other lines the poet affirms that this Byzantine illumination can teach "One of the things at least that
life must mean, / And standing in the book of days a
splen- / did summary, rubric, index of the end"; this red and
gold leaf is an emblem "with instruction how to die."
      The poem ends with what seems to be an anti-climax, or
at least an idea that does not so much complete this poem as
start another one. What the last couple of lines say is true, of
course, that the first leaf that dies is the first to acquire
immortality, but "turncoat" and "Judas sheep" seem inap-
propriate. Perhaps Nemerov could not resist the joke and the
opportunity of punning with "turncoat."
      Dandelions are another occasion for reflection about the
natural teleology. In the first eight lines of "Dandelions"
(SG) the speaker is struck by "these golden heads" that are
numerous and "shine as lovely as they're mean." But the
present tense of the golden dandelions quickly becomes the
future in the imagination of the poet. The last twenty lines of
the poem are surely poignant, laden with the same sense of
loss that one can find in Wordsworth:

Inside a week they will be seen
Stricken and old, ghosts in the field
To be picked up at the lightest breath,
With brazen tops all shrunken in
And swollen green gone withered white.
You'll say it's nature's price for beauty
That goes cheap; that being light
Is justly what makes girls grow heavy;
And that the wind, bearing their death,
Whispers the second kingdom come.
—You'll say, the fool of piety,
By resignations hanging on
Until, still justified, you drop.
But surely the thing is sorrowful,
At evening, when the light goes out
Slowly, to see those ruined spinsters,
All down the field their ghostly hair,
Dry sinners waiting in the valley
For the last word and the next life
And the liberation from the lion's mouth.

One element of the poem that Wordsworth likely would not have included (or risked) is the witty observation "that being light / Is justly what makes girls grow heavy," but I think this is an instance where the wit works quite well. Just as Donne's wit works in his poetry.

Death as the anagoge takes several forms, and sometimes the effect is frightening and terrible (as it is not in "Dandelions," "Midsummer's Day," and "The First Leaf"). Two poems illustrate what I have in mind. One is "Between the Window and the Screen" from *The Blue Swallows*.

Between the window and the screen
A black fly climbed and fell
All day, then toward nightfall
Despaired and died.

Next morning there one tiny ant
Raced up and down the screen

Holding above his head
That huge black hulk.

I helped not, nor oversaw the end
Ordained to the black ant
Bearing the thin-winged heavy death
Aloft as a proud flag,

But write it out for you to read
And take what it may yield;
No harder emblem had
Achilles' shield.

Death here is death of the predator and the scavenger. It is
the kind of death which is so much more frightening because
it reminds us of our own existence, that we too live on the
death of plants and other animals. Joel Conarroe, after having
noted that Nemerov had addressed a moving poem to Robert
Frost ("For Robert Frost, in the Autumn in Vermont"),
writes that "There is also an implicit tribute [to Frost], in
'Between the Window and the Screen,' which describes an ant
holding a dead fly's wing above his head, and is thus a sort of
ebony 'Design'."[7] While agreeing about the implicit tribute,
one might observe that there is no reason to interpret the
lines to mean holding a dead fly's wing above his head, as the
lines read "holding above his head / That huge black hulk."
Later in the poem the ant holds aloft "the thin-winged heavy
death" which I presume includes the whole fly. But this
matter is not worth a fly perhaps. Conarroe's main observation is appropriate, though. In addition, there may be several
possible associations that the poet makes with this scene and
an emblem on Achilles' shield. There are many designs on the
shield, certainly, and some of them dark. One of them, one
recalls, pictures a warrior dragging a corpse through the
crowd. Then, too, Achilles drags Hector about. Maybe a little
too ingenious is the concern of Achilles that if he leaves to
kill Hector, there will be no one to keep the flies away from

7. Conarroe, "Visions and Revisions," in Duncan (ed.), *The Critical Reception of Howard Nemerov*, 141.

his friend Patroclus' corpse (Thetis assuring him that she will).
Unquiet death that is terrible and frightening is also found
in "These Words Also" (*NRD*). The speaker has apparently
chanced on what might be a letter from his wife's mother
who is in turn writing about a girl, or even another daughter.
The exact details may not matter, but what does matter is
the section of the letter the sunlight causes to stand out:
" 'After a night of drink and too much talk, / After the
casual companions had gone home, / She did this. . . .' " A
characteristic turning of the poet's mind to his choice of
analogy is illuminating here. The analogy is quite dark, although there are strange beauties even in the darkness.

> The garden holds its sunlight heavy and still
> As if in a gold frame around the flowers
> That nod and never change, the picture-book
> Flowers of somebody's forbidden childhood,
> Pale lemony lilies, pansies with brilliant scowls
> Pretending to be children. Only they live,
> And it is beautiful enough, to live,
> Having to do with hunger and reflection,
> A matter of thresholds, of thoughtless balancings.
>
> The black and gold morning goes on, and
> What is a girl's life? There on the path
> Red ants are pulling a shiny beetle along
> Through the toy kingdom where nobody thinks.

Sudden, unanticipated death may cause several responses and
one certainly may be to affirm what is possible, minimal
though it might be: "And it is beautiful enough, to live." But
for those who are not inveterate optimists, a dark counterpoint to this affirmation may accompany it—instead of affirmation, a question. "What is a girl's life? There on the
path / Red ants are pulling a shiny beetle along / Through
the toy kingdom where nobody thinks."
These curious twins of beauty and death occupy an
important place in Nemerov's mental landscape and reveal his

permanent convictions. That these two facts, beauty and death, exist may be the root of the impulsion to write in the first place. The poet has said as much in an address before the National Poetry Festival. His final sentence in that address was, "We write, at last, because life is hopeless and beautiful."[8] This same attitude is found in a poem that is often read by people in public performances and is a moving experience: "The View from an Attic Window" (NSP). The first section of the poem relates how the speaker, standing at an attic window, watches the leafless trees and the falling snow. Something in the common occurrence of these two things moves him and he says that he cried and fell asleep, only to wake in the darkness of night. The second section of the poem is an "explanation," or reflection on this experience:

> I cried because life is hopeless and beautiful.
> And like a child I cried myself to sleep
> High in the head of the house, feeling the hull
> Beneath me pitch and roll among the steep
> Mountains and valleys of the many years
>   Which brought me to tears.
>
> Down in the cellar, furnace and washing machine,
> Pump, fuse-box, water heater, work their hearts
> Out at my life, which narrowly runs between
> Them and this cemetery of spare parts
> For discontinued men, whose hats and canes
>   Are my rich remains.
>
> And women, their portraits and wedding gowns
> Stacked in the corners, brooding in wooden trunks;
> And children's rattles, books about lions and clowns;
> And headless, hanging dresses swayed like drunks
> Whenever a living footstep shakes the floor;
>   I mention no more;

8. Nemerov, *Poetry and Fiction: Essays,* 47.

But what I thought today, that made me cry,
Is this, that we live in two kinds of things:
The powerful trees, thrusting into the sky
Their black patience, are one, and that branching
Relation teaches how we endure and grow;
   The other is the snow,

Falling in a white chaos from the sky,
As many as the sands of all the seas,
As all the men who died or who will die,
As stars in heaven, as leaves of all the trees;
As Abraham was promised of his seed;
   Generations bleed,

Till I, high in the tower of my time
Among familiar ruins, began to cry
For accident, sickness, justice, war and crime,
Because all died, because I had to die.
The snow fell, the trees stood, the promise kept,
   And a child I slept.

This is the vision of the attentive and obedient poet. As he
listens and watches the world outside, he does not flinch and
deny either the beauty of life and growth in the face of the
snow, and death, nor does the splendor of the beautiful blind
him to the inevitable. "The snow fell, the trees stood," but
also "the promise kept," recalling the promise to Abraham
that his descendants would be many and blessed.

5

The Urban Landscape

Nemerov's poetry divides itself between contemplative poetry, which most often springs from his encounter with nature, and satiric poetry that finds its nourishment in disparities and paradoxes that reveal themselves in the urban scene. To say that the poetry is divided in subject matter and concern is not, however, to say that the poet is divided. These disparities and paradoxes are revealed by a vision that knows the difference in authentic and inauthentic existence, and knows the call of conscience. This vision knows that for someone to say there is a boom in religion because of increased affluence is to hear what Heidegger calls "idle talk."

> And because this discoursing has lost its primary relationship-of-Being towards the entity talked about, or else has never achieved such a relationship, it does not communicate in such a way as to let this entity be appropriated in a primordial manner, but communicates rather by following the route of *gossiping* and *passing the word along*. What is said-in-the-talk as such, spreads in wider circles and takes on an authoritative character. Things are so because one says so. . . .[1]

1. Martin Heidegger, *Being and Time*, tr. John Macquarrie and Edward Robinson (New York: Harper & Row, 1962), 212.

119

Language of idle talk, since it does not mirror a primary relationship to what is being talked about, mirrors nothing. It only seems to mirror something, and so "takes on an authoritative character." As this kind of talk becomes public and authoritative, the inauthentic self seems released from the task of genuine understanding. "Because of this, idle talk discourages any new inquiry and any disputation, and in a peculiar way suppresses them and holds them back," continues Heidegger, in *Being and Time*.[2] This kind of talk corresponds to what Nemerov calls "verbal effigies," of which we will hear more shortly.

The disparities and paradoxes that Nemerov reveals through his authentic vision often take the form of jokes—so say some of the critics, disparagingly, and so says Nemerov, but with an explanation.

It sometimes seems to me as though our relations with the Devil have reached that place, so near the end, where paradox appears immediately in all phenomena, so that, for example, the increase of life is the fated increase of mortal suffering, the multiplication of the means of communication is the multiplication of meaninglessness, and so on. At the obsequies for the late President of the United States the "eternal flame" was extinguished by holy water in the hands of children; in the material world that may have been an unfortunate accident, but in the poetic world, where one is compelled to listen to symbolic things, it appears as possibly a final warning, a witty and indeed diabolical underlining of the dire assassination itself.

So if paradox and accenting the hidden side of the paradoxical has always played such a part in my poetry, perhaps the seriousness of that view of life, its necessity even, may now begin to appear. The charge typically raised

2. *Ibid.*, 213.

against my work by literary critics has been
that my poems are jokes, even bad jokes. I
incline to agree, insisting however that they
are bad jokes, and even terrible jokes, emerg-
ing from the nature of things as well as from
my propensity for coming at things a touch
subversively and from the blind side, or the
dark side, the side everyone concerned with
"values" would just as soon forget.[3]

Even though there appears to be a division in the body of the
poet's work, he at least sees a unity.

Principally, in this chapter, I would like to take note of
Nemerov's urban landscape: the parts that make him laugh,
even if it means a subsequent kick in the stomach, and the
parts that make him quietly rage. Often, as I have noted, the
observations take the form of some kind of joke, though
certainly this is not always so.

A number of the poems that embody jokes are grouped
in a section of *The Blue Swallows* called "The Great Society." The second poem of the group illustrates a persistent
ironic quality of this part of Nemerov's work.

SUNDAY

He rested on the seventh day, and so
The chauffeur had the morning off, the maid
Slept late, and the cook went out to morning mass.
So by and large there was nothing to do
Among the ashtrays in the living room
But breathe the greyish air left over from
Last night, and go down on your knees to read
The horrible funnies flattened on the floor.

It's still a day to conjure with, if not
Against, the blessed seventh, when we get
A chance to feel whatever He must feel,

3. Nemerov, *Reflexions on Poetry and Poetics*, 170.

Looking us over, seeing that we are good.
The odds are six to one He's gone away;
It's why there's so much praying on this day.

The setting is familiar in modern poetry, a Sunday on which the character or characters are not taking part in the ritual of the culture. Eliot's "Mr. Eliot's Sunday Morning Service" and Wallace Stevens' "Sunday Morning" are of course the most famous of such poems and much more elaborate than Nemerov's. In addition, Stevens' goes on to a kind of affirmation that is not evident in Nemerov's. In this one "the odds are six to one He's gone away." Perhaps, the speaker muses, we feel similar to God, since both of us are resting on the seventh day, but he suspects God is not in God's house as he is in his.

There are several senses in which this poet can be described as "religious," although not in a conventional way. If a deep concern for the world and even for metaphysics is religious, then truly Nemerov is. But it is also true that he persistently takes his shots at organized religion. For instance, consider "Debate with the Rabbi" (*NRD*):

You've lost your religion, the Rabbi said.
    It wasn't much to keep, said I.
You should affirm the spirit, said he,
And the communal solidarity.
    I don't feel so solid, I said.
We are the people of the Book, the Rabbi said.
    Not of the phone book, said I.
Ours is a great tradition, said he,
And a wonderful history.
    But history's over, I said.

We Jews are creative people, the Rabbi said.
    Make something, then, said I.
In science and in art, said he,
Violinists and physicists have we.
    Fiddle and physic indeed, I said.

> Stubborn and stiff-necked man! the Rabbi cried.
> The pain you give me, said I.
> Instead of bowing down, said he,
> You go on in your obstinacy.
> We Jews are that way, I replied.

Although the idea behind the poem is a serious one, this may well be described as "light verse." If such verse were the sole achievement of the poet, it would not be enough to create the reputation that he has. With this said, it can be observed that such verse complements his lyric voice and makes a different kind of statement. The rabbi's opponent will not be persuaded by categorical imperatives that he does not feel. He cannot affirm a "communal solidarity" because he does not "feel so solid." This play on words offers a kind of revelation that Nemerov is quick to point out shares a commonality with the lyric. His essay "Bottom's Dream: The Likeness of Poems and Jokes" explores this commonality.

> ...one mechanism of economy in joking is the pun, either in the use of one word in two senses ... or in the use of two words of similar sound which mean different things but still somehow establish a resemblance beyond that of the sound.

Concerning jokes he says:

> A joke expresses tension, which it releases in laughter; it is a sort of permissible rebellion against things as they are—permissible, perhaps, because this rebellion is at the same time stoically resigned, it acknowledges that things are as they are, and that they will, after the moment of laughter, continue to be that way. That is why jokes concentrate on the

most sensitive areas of human concern: sex,
death, religion, and the most powerful institutions of society; and poems do the same.[4]

Accordingly, the rabbi's opponent says he does not feel solid,
either in his belief or in his hunch about himself and the
world; thus, he is unable to affirm "communal solidarity."
The rabbi attempts to entice by an appeal to tradition, but
his opponent insists that history is over, which it obviously is;
but less obviously, the opponent thinks, the past should not
tyrannize the present, an omnipresent theme of Nemerov.

As Nemerov searches the modern terrain he insists that
"bad jokes, even terrible jokes" emerge from the nature of
things and the nature of the "Great Society." In a vein that
sustains this criticism of the contemporary church, he has
written a poem called "Boom!" (NSP) which was inspired by
the daily newspaper. The passage in the Associated Press
release that struck Nemerov was the following.

Atlantic City, June 23, 1957 (AP).—President
Eisenhower's pastor said tonight that Americans are living in a period of "unprecedented
religious activity" caused partially by paid
vacations, the eight-hour day and modern
conveniences.

"These fruits of material progress," said the
Rev. Edward L. R. Elson of the National
Presbyterian Church, Washington, "have pro-
vided the leisure, the energy, and the means
for a level of human and spiritual values never
before reached."

The idea of opulence leading to spiritual values—values that
had their origin in austerity, pain, and suffering—jars the
poet's sensibilities. The poem begins:

4. Ibid., 12.

Here at the Vespasian-Carlton, it's just one
religious activity after another; the sky
is constantly being crossed by cruciform
airplanes, in which nobody disbelieves
for a second, and the tide, the tide
of spiritual progress and prosperity
miraculously keeps rising, to a level
never before attained. The churches are full,
the beaches are full, and the filling-stations
are full, God's great ocean is full
of paid vacationers praying an eight-hour day
to the human and spiritual values, the fruits,
the leisure, the energy, and the means, Lord,
the means for the level, the unprecedented level,
and the modern conveniences, which also are full.

The effect of asserting that the "churches are full" is rapidly
neutralized by noting that everything else is full. Besides
beaches and filling-stations, all the modern conveniences are
full, with the suggestion that a particular convenience that we
fill daily is now running over—with much the same substance
as the minister's observations. The poem, of some forty-five
lines, continues to build up details of the affluent society,
but midway through the poet notes tersely: "It was not thus
when Job in Palestine / sat In the dust and cried, cried
bitterly." Nemerov would insist that if there are "jokes" in
his poems, surely there is a horrible joke in the reality of the
daily newspaper article.

Observations like those of the minister—repetitiously
presented in the mass media—become increasingly dangerous,
because their very repetition transforms them into dogma.
This is the language of "idle talk," mirroring nothing but
seeming to, and as such, taking on authoritative character.
In addition, it keeps us from further inquiry. Nemerov
explores this danger:

The thought of statues as representing a false,
historical immortality seems clearly related to

the scriptural prohibition against the making
of graven images; and the category in which
the statues finally come, which I generalized
out as "effigies," may include also photographs, mythological figures such as Santa
Claus, even mannequins in shop windows, or
anything that tends to confirm the mind in a
habitual way of regarding the world, which
habitual way is, to be short with it, idolatry.
There are many examples in my work, and I
have chosen one which represents newspapers,
by a slight extension of the thought, as a sort
of verbal effigy, idolatrously confirming
human beings day after day in the habit of a
mean delusion and compelling them to regard
this mean delusion as their sole reality. I say
this halfway as a joke with the name of a
newspaper, *The Daily Globe.*[5]

The poem "The Daily Globe" (*NRD*) elaborates his criticism:

Each day another installment of the old
Romance of Order brings to the breakfast table
The paper flowers of catastrophe.
One has this recurrent dream about the world.

Headlines declare the ambiguous oracles,
The comfortable old prophets mutter doom.
Man's greatest intellectual pleasure is
To repeat himself, yet somehow the daily globe

Rolls on, while the characters in comic strips
Prolong their slow, interminable lives
Beyond the segregated photographs
Of the girls that marry and the men that die.

5. *Ibid.,* 170–71.

Nemerov says that for the benefit of foreign audiences he would point out that obituary pages in this country are almost exclusively of men and the matrimonial pages exclusively of women. Nemerov thinks that such habitual ways of regarding the world, described in the poem, are on the increase. One of the functions of the poet then is to help man see the world freshly. One way that poets have always done this is by holding up a mirror so that man may see himself, his own nature and the nature that is outside him. Nemerov notes that "if my poetry does envision the appearance of a new human nature, it does so chiefly in sarcastic outrage, for that new human nature appears in the poetry merely as a totalitarian fixing of the old human nature, whose principal products have been anguish, war, and history."[6] Nemerov's satiric mirror helps man to see himself as he is, and the mirror held up to nature puts him in touch with the currents of being.

Nemerov has noted that makers of jokes and smart remarks resemble poets in another way in that they would also be "excluded from Plato's Republic; for it is of the nature of Utopia and the Crystal Palace, as Dostoevsky said, that you can't stick your tongue out at it."[7] Turning from the church to politics, I might select three or four short instances where the poet's tongue is showing.[8]

No bars are set too close, no mesh too fine
To keep me from the eagle and the lion,
Whom keepers feed that I may freely dine.
This goes to show that if you have the wit
To be small, common, cute, and live on shit,
Though the cage fret kings, you may make free with it.

6. *Ibid.,* 171.
7. *Ibid.,* 12.
8. The first such example was published in *Mirrors and Windows* as part of a series of "Epigrams" and was called "VI Political Reflexion, loquitur the sparrow in the zoo." Later when it was collected in the *New and Selected,* it was given the title "The Sparrow in the Zoo."

So much for the lower end of the political scene, with its hangers-on and opportunists.

Another poem, "The Iron Characters" (*NRD*), in one way takes up the other end of the political spectrum, but part of its theme is a kind of commonality that is shared by the great and small.

> The iron characters, keepers of the public
>   confidence,
> The sponsors, fund raisers, and members of
>   the board,
> Who naturally assume their seats among the
>   governors,
> Who place their names behind the issue of
>   bonds
> And are consulted in the formation of
>   cabinets,
> The catastrophes of war, depression, and
>   natural disaster:
> They represent us in responsibilities many and
>   great.
> It is no wonder, then, if in a moment of crisis,
> Before the microphones, under the lights, on
>   a great occasion,
> One of them will break down in hysterical
>   weeping
> Or fall in an epileptic seizure, or if one day
> We read in the papers of one's having been
>   found
> Naked and drunk in a basement with three
>   high school boys,
> Or one who jumped from the window of his
>   hospital room.
> For are they not as ourselves in these things
>   also?
> Let the orphan, the pauper, the thief, the
>   derelict drunk
> And all those of no fixed address, shed tears
>   of rejoicing

> For the broken minds of the strong, the torn
> flesh of the just.

There is a tension of sentiment in the poem that insists on our reflection here. The "iron characters" do represent us in responsibilities and because this is so, they are the "keepers of the public confidence." When Nemerov selects certain very pathetic and awful moments when the keepers of the confidence break, it is not with malice. In only one instance might the newspaper reader feel occasioned to laugh: at the figure found naked and drunk with high school boys, because our nervous attitude about sexual mystery quickly finds its outlet in some kind of laughter—sometimes. It may be the case of Profumo in England or of Senator Kennedy in the United States. But these are "horrible jokes" that are no jokes. Thus, there is an obvious sympathy in the selection of examples. On the other hand, there is an ironic pleasure or affirmation for "all those of no fixed address" when they discover that the mighty are made of flesh also. Surely It Is ironic that the orphan and the pauper should shed "tears of rejoicing / For the broken minds of the strong, the torn flesh of the just." The "tears of rejoicing" are shed simply because of a commonality or brotherhood that becomes apparent when the characters cease being "iron" and appear as all too human.

"To the Governor & Legislature of Massachusetts" (*BS*) is turned out with a livelier hand than the preceding poem, and incidentally reflects a part of recent Americana—that following the McCarthy era and the great Communist scare. University professors, among many others, found themselves being forced to sign "security oaths" and to promise that they would not overthrow the government. Apparently this happened to Nemerov:

> When I took a job teaching in Massachusetts
> I didn't know and no one told me that I'd
>   have to sign
> An oath of loyalty to the Commonwealth of
>   Massachusetts.

Now that I'm hooked, though, with a house
And a mortgage on the house, the road ahead
Is clear: I sign. But I want you gentlemen to
    know
That till today it never once occurred to me
To overthrow the Commonwealth of
    Massachusetts
By violence or subversion, or by preaching
    either.
But now I'm not so sure. It makes a fellow
    think,
Can such things be? Can such things be in the
    very crib
Of our liberties, and East of the Hudson, at
    that?

So if the day come that I should shove the
    Berkshire Hills
Over the border and annex them to Vermont,
Or snap Cape Cod off at the elbow and scatter
Hyannis to Provincetown beyond the twelve-
    mile limit,
Proclaiming apocalypsopetls to my pupils
And with state troopers dripping from my
    fingertips
Squeaking "You promised, you broke your
    promise!"
You gentlemen just sit there with my
    signature
And keep on lawyer-talking like nothing had
    happened,
Lest I root out that wagon tongue on Bunker
    Hill
And fungo your Golden Dome right into
    Fenway Park
Like any red-celled American boy ought to
    done
Long ago in the first place, just to keep in
    practice.

Perhaps incidental to the poem, there is here an example of Nemerov as liberal, which he certainly is. Though he handles the theme with wild hyperbole, there is a reasonable degree of serious anger. This is another occasion of the bad jokes that he insists constantly emerge from the contemporary ruins.

In the early 1950s when the United States was much troubled by the fear of Communist infiltrators, an economist for the U.S. Commerce Department, William Remington, was sentenced to three years for perjury, for denying he had given secret data to a Russian spy ring. Scheduled for release in August 1955 he was beaten to death by two fellow inmates in late November 1954. There was speculation that he had been beaten because of anti-Communist sentiment within the inmate population of the Lewisburg, Pennsylvania, prison. Nemerov reacts to the brutality of the killing (the murderers used a brick inside a sock) in "The Murder of William Remington" (MW), reflecting about the function of law and punishment, and that much punishment may be a grim joke the majority play on the few.

> There is the terror too of each man's thought,
> That knows not, but must quietly suspect
> His neighbor, friend, or self of being taught
> To take an attitude merely correct;
> Being frightened of his own cold image in
> The glass of government, and his own sin,
>
> Frightened lest senate house and prison wall
> Be quarried of one stone, lest righteous and high
> Look faintly smiling down and seem to call
> A crime the welcome chance of liberty,
> And any man an outlaw who aggrieves
> The patriotism of a pair of thieves.

"The Great Society, Mark X" (BS) picks up the phrase that was coined during the Johnson years, years that signaled to Americans that there may be rents in the fabric of their society. The affluence following World War II seemed to create as many problems as it solved, or it may have simply given Americans the leisure to reflect on them. Ralph Nader came along during the years of "The Great Society" with his exposé of General Motors. It may also be that since the assembly line, with its association of Ford's Model T, helped to usher in the era of mass production that gives a foundation to the present affluent society, it is appropriate that Nemerov chooses an automobile which is falling apart to embody the erosion of the society.

> The engine and transmission and the wheels
> Are made of greed, fear, and invidiousness
> Fueled by super-pep high octane money
> And lubricated with hypocrisy,
> Interior upholstery is all handsewn
> Of the skins of children of the very poor,
> Justice and mercy, charity and peace,
> Are optional items at slight extra cost,
> The steering gear is newspring powered by
> Expediency but not connected with
> The wheels, and finally there are no brakes.
>
> However, the rear-view mirror and the horn
> Are covered by our lifetime guarantee.

The criticism of the society in this poem has been heard with much greater frequency in the intervening years, as, some feel, the wealth continues to accumulate in the hands of the powerful few. This is the articulated voice of a liberal. "Interior upholstery is all handsewn / Of the skins of children of the very poor," is a bit melodramatic, but the last three lines are, I think, the most haunting. A contemporary American despair derives from the fear that there is no way of stopping the juggernaut, that "there are no brakes." It is yet to be seen whether the "automobile" can be steered by anything but expediency, or whether the machine will have to be destroyed and a new one built. Two things are guaranteed: there is a rear-view mirror through which we can see the wreckage-strewn past and see where we have been, and a frightening horn that can only blow, hoping everyone will get out of the way. All in all, this is a terrible, mad-cap machine.

The poet continues to examine the nature of greed, invidiousness, and injustice in "Money" (BS). The figure he examines is the "buffalo" nickel that is now out of circulation. As Nemerov recalls for us, there was a standing buffalo on one side and the face of an Indian on the other. As for the buffalo, "one side shows a hunchbacked bison / Bending his head and curling his tail to accommodate / The circular nature of money." The main effect of this is to accentuate the overpowering influence of money but it is another reminder of the way greed and unawareness "influenced" the buffalo almost right out of existence. By extension, modern industrial society has temporarily made the natural world "accommodate" itself to a very demanding will. Temporarily, because as we are now aware, it was with a price that we may not be able to pay back.

As to the figure of the Indian:

> And on the other side of our nickel
> There is the profile of a man with long hair
> And a couple of feathers in the hair; we know
> Somehow that he is an American Indian, and
> He wears the number nineteen-thirty-six.
> Right in front of his eyes the word *LIBERTY*, bent
> To conform with the curve of the rim, appears
> To be falling out of the sky Y first; the Indian
> Keeps his eyes downcast and does not notice this;

Wearing the number nineteen-thirty-six has the association of a prisoner, which of course the Indian was and to some extent continues to be; at the same time there is the association of "his days are numbered" or at least his numbers are scarce. Right before the Indian's eyes, the nature of money "bends" or perverts any real notion of liberty. In just one or two lines the poet reminds us of much of our American past that we are not proud of; and he helps to clarify what many have known about one kind of *laissez faire*—that it often means "Devil-take-the-hindmost."

This poem is also an example of the danger any poet runs, and that is over-writing, or once something has been said, to then take up the expansive process of prose and continue to explain. The passage I have just excerpted was quite enough, I think. But Nemerov goes on to explain,

> The representative American Indian was destroyed
> A hundred years or so ago, and his descendants'
> Relations with liberty are maintained with
>   reservations,
> Or primitive concentration camps.

While not commenting specifically on this poem, Miller Williams has noted in a review of *Blue Swallows,* from which "Money" is taken, that "While the beginnings and resolutions of almost all Nemerov's poems are as tight as good craftsmanship can make them, a number have a curious way of going loose in rhythm and almost rambling in the middle, so that the reader has the feeling of crossing a suspension bridge. These are faults, if I read fairly; but they are moved over without serious stumbling, and sometimes are no more than the peculiar mark of the man."[9] The passage from "Money" supports this contention.

My own hunch is that this sort of thing occurs more frequently in the satiric poetry about the contemporary urban scene than it does with the more meditative poetry. This may be because abstract ideologies (political or otherwise) are more difficult to turn into poetic images than the insights that Nature may provide.

In addition to areas of the church, the state, and war (which are amply treated in the early volumes), there are

---

9. Miller Williams, "Transactions with the Muse," in Bowie Duncan (ed.), *The Critical Reception of Howard Nemerov*, 144.

several poems that reflect his attitudes about race. The first, an example of the terrible jokes that present themselves to the poet and which he continues to joke about, in a serious way, is entitled "A Negro Cemetery Next to a White One" (*BS*).

> I wouldn't much object, if I were black,
> To being turned away at the iron gate
> By the dark blonde angel holding up a plaque
> That said White Only; who would mind the wait
>
> For those facilities? And still it's odd,
> Though a natural god-given civil right,
> For men to throw it in the face of God
> Some ghosts are black and some darknesses white.
>
> But since they failed to integrate the earth,
> It's white of them to give what tantamounts
> To it, making us all, for what that's worth,
> Separate but equal where it counts.

After musing on the anomaly of a Christian turning another human being away because of color, the poet turns the situation further on its head and with irony by inversion observes that the earth is integrated surely in the end as the elements mix themselves and where no one's elements are separate, though truly they are equal.

The poem "A Picture" (*NRD*) engages the racial problem in another way and the revelation of this poem is I think of a profounder order. The scene, from a photo in a newspaper, is the image of a group of people running down a city street after something; the first part of the poem isolates several of the people with comment, one a man in a "fat white shirt" who is "dutifully / Running along with all the others," and then:

> The running faces did not record
> Hatred or anger or great enthusiasm

For what they were doing (hunting down
A Negro, according to the caption),
But seemed rather solemn, intent,
With the serious patience of animals
Driven through a gate by some
Urgency out of the camera's range,
On an occasion too serious
For private feeling. The breathless faces
Expressed a religion of running,
A form of ritual exaltation
Devoted to obedience, and
Obedient, it might be, to the Negro,
Who was not caught by the camera
When it took the people in the street
Among the cars, toward some object,
Seriously running.

So much of the powerful inherited legacy of Man the animal, Man the descendant of *australopithecus africanus,* is rendered in this very haunting scene. The ritual of running is acted out as a matter of great solemnity, in the way a pack of hounds follows its prey with single-mindedness, a community effort. In the way that hounds are "driven," although they seem to drive, the people are "Devoted to obedience, and / Obedient, it might be, to the Negro, / Who was not caught by the camera." The poet's intelligence roves the contemporary landscape, in this instance an urban one, discovering strange rents in the fabric of civilization, rents that often appear to resemble bad jokes.

Another poem concerning race (of course all these poems embody more than a racial theme) but which does not fall into the category of jokes is "The Sweeper of Ways" (*BS*). The poet himself has written about the poem in his last collection of essays. The occasion for the poem was one of his habitual meetings with a Negro man who swept the sidewalk of leaves at a school where they both worked. Part of the poem reflects a middle-class, liberal embarrassment that anyone has to work at menial jobs because of his background and not because of his potential. The speaker reflects:

> Masters, we carry our white faces by
> In silent prayer, Don't hate me, on a wave-
> length which his broom's antennae perfectly
> Pick up, we know ourselves so many thoughts
> Considered by a careful, kindly mind
> Which can do nothing, and is doing that.

Nemerov has commented that "This kindly old man exempli-
fies a wrong in society. I didn't do it, but I have to feel
responsible. And I detest about society this constant en-
forcing upon its members feelings of responsibility which are
also deeply hopeless and despairing, so that one guilt evokes
another, without remedy or end. For even if you could
correct the future, what about the past? Many thousands
gone."[10] And the poet is mightily impressed with the patience and apparent lack of bitterness.

Three other poems gradually pull back from specific
areas of man's experience until the perspective is quite wide.
The first of these, "Cybernetics" (*BS*), is directed to someone
who is ready to build a human brain, but in substance the
poem is much more about the nature of man and his history.
There is only profound, respectful admiration for man's
complexity and his capabilities. The poet notes that for a
cyberneticist to make a human brain, he would have to start
with an area as big as Central Park and it would cost a little
more than the Nineteen Fifty-Nine Gross National Product.
He continues to enumerate many other problems the cyberneticist will have as he goes about his project. He observes,
not resisting the pun, that the brain "must, of course, be
absolutely free, / That's been determined." In the midst of
its freedom, it is threatened with "yesterday's disasters" and
must at the same time "assure itself, by masterful / Ad-
ministration of the unforeseen, / That everything works according to plan." Out of the tension may be achieved that
which permits man to endure: "something between / The
flood of power and the drouth of fear: / A mediocrity, or
golden mean, / Maybe at best the stoic *apatheia*." Further,

---

10. Nemerov, *Reflexions on Poetry and Poetics,* 163.

if one intends to build a brain, he must install a "limiting tradition, / Which may be simple and parochial / (A memory of Main Street in the sunlight)" and the tradition should be as unequivocal as " 'God will punish me if I suck my thumb.' "

If the brain-maker wants something rather elaborate, he can have it, but he must understand that this could be expensive.

> It runs you into much more money for
> Circuits of paradox and contradiction.
> Your vessels of antinomian wrath alone
> Run into millions; and you can't stop there,
> You've got to add at every junction point
> Auxiliary systems that will handle doubt,
> Switches of agony that are On and Off
> At the same time, and limited-access
> Blind alleys full of inefficient gods
> And marvelous devils.

And in the closing section of the poem, the speaker addresses the budding cyberneticist with irony that may be appropriate to someone who is now taking on the powers of Creator.

> O helmsman! in your hands how equal now
> Weigh opportunity and obligation.
> A chance to mate those monsters of the Book,
> The lion and serpent hidden from our sight
> Through centuries of shadowed speculation.
> What if the Will's a baffled, mangy lion,
> Or Thought's no adder but a strong constrictor?
> It is their offspring that we care about,
> That marvelous mirror where our modest wit
> Shall show gigantic. Will he uproot cities,
> Or sit indoors on a rainy day and mope?
> Will he decide against us, or want love?
> How shall we see him, or endure his stride

> Into our future bellowing Nil Mirari
> While all his circuits click, propounding new
> Solutions to the riddle of the Sphinx?

Some reviewers have commented on Nemerov's negativism, or in Meinke's words his "minimal affirmation." But over and over again Nemerov emphatically affirms man, and to use his own words, he is a poet who has "got so far as to believe in the existence of the world."[11] This is not the same thing as saying that he sentimentalizes the goodness of man and neglects man the beast. But who would believe a poet, or take him seriously, if he did offer such a sweeping, uncritical "affirmation"? "Cybernetics" is just such a poem that admits man's fantastic complexity and yet tacitly admires the courage he does show in the face of what he must confront. The poet chides the budding scientist for not being aware of just what he may be embarking on, and in so doing Nemerov affirms man. Nemerov affirms man in all his possibilities, authentic and inauthentic. It is man, and only man, who has the possibility of a relationship to being, who in his freedom can care, who can hear the call of conscience (Heidegger's *Dasein*). Just in what way the full ramifications of all of this can be labeled "minimal affirmation" is difficult to see.

"A Primer of the Daily Round" (*MW*) does not require any explication, it makes its statement clearly enough, but It is a delightful short poem and ends, to use a word that one has to use often with Nemerov, hauntingly.

> A peels an apple, while B kneels to God,
> C telephones to D, who has a hand
> On E's knee, F coughs, G turns up the sod
> for H's grave, I do not understand
> But J is bringing one clay pigeon down
> While K brings down a nightstick on L's head,
> and M takes mustard, N drives into town,

---

11. Nemerov, *Poetry and Fiction: Essays,* 3.

O goes to bed with P, and Q drops dead,
R lies to S, but happens to be heard
by T, who tells U not to fire V
For having to give W the word
That X is now deceiving Y with Z,
    Who happens just now to remember A
Peeling an apple somewhere far away.

The last two lines reinforce Miller Williams' comment that the "resolutions of almost all Nemerov's poems are as tight as good craftsmanship can make them "[12]   This poem, along with the next, is often selected for public readings; both lend themselves to a first hearing.

"Life Cycle of Common Man" (*NSP*) is specifically about the "average consumer of the middle class." Nemerov estimates some of the consumables, ("Just under half a million cigarettes, / Four thousand fifths of gin and about / A quarter as much vermouth"), and the cost of putting him through life, his parents' investment and "how many beasts / Died to provide him with meat, belt and shoes / Cannot be certainly said." He pictures the man leaving a long trail of waste behind him. What did he do?

                    The usual things, of course,
The eating, dreaming, drinking and begetting,
And he worked for the money which was to pay
For the eating, et cetera, which were necessary
If he were to go on working for the money, et cetera,
But chiefly he talked. As the bottles and bones
Accumulated behind him the words proceeded
Steadily from the front of his face as he
Advanced into the silence and made it verbal.

There were countless greetings and good-byes, gratitudes, and "statements beginning 'It seems to me' or 'As I always say.' " The poem closes with a lonely figure, strangely modern.

12. Williams, "Transactions with the Muse," 144.

Consider the courage in all that, and behold the man
Walking into deep silence, with the ectoplastic
Cartoon's balloon of speech proceeding
Steadily out of the front of his face, the words
Borne along on the breath which is his spirit
Telling the numberless tale of his untold Word
Which makes the world his apple, and forces him
    to eat.

This is the kind of affirmation that Nemerov makes, affirming the kind of courage that modern man must have in order
to face a world that "forces him to eat."

One final poem, a very delicate and poignant poem,
evokes the poet's stance and describes the kind of courage
that a sensitive mind must possess to face the often dark,
terrifying world.

To D_____, Dead by Her Own Hand

My dear, I wonder if before the end
You ever thought about a children's game—
I'm sure you must have played it too—in which
You ran along a narrow garden wall
Pretending it to be a mountain ledge
So steep a snowy darkness fell away
On either side to deeps invisible;
And when you felt your balance being lost
You jumped because you feared to fall, and thought
For only an instant: That was when I died.

That was a life ago. And now you've gone,
Who would no longer play the grown-ups' game
Where, balanced on the ledge above the dark,
You go on running and you don't look down,
Nor ever jump because you fear to fall. (G&O)

The courage is perhaps an act of faith, or else a result of
having nothing else to do or lose. One walks along the edge of

what separates the known (or what we think we know) and what we know we do not know, the edge of order and chaos, of hope and despair. But, "you go on running."

In this survey of the poems about man and his city-societies there emerges a liberal mind, in this case a particularly civilized and witty mind, which responds to what it sees. What Nemerov chooses to single out for comment and what is manifestly part of his uniqueness, comes from his talent for recognizing the paradoxes and bad jokes inherent in the most sensitive areas of human concern. The poetry that reflects the urban landscape concentrates on the most powerful institutions of society. Nemerov is particularly concerned with the tyranny of the past over the present—a tyranny which is manifest in the way it compels habitual action and habitual ways of looking at the world, whether it is the equation of greater numbers in church with a spiritual awakening, the customary selection of males for the obituary page and females for the matrimonial page, or the ritual force of our racial prejudices. As is true of all satire, there is affirmation, some assertion of value, and this is certainly true of Nemerov's. The poet helps us see the world freshly and, in so doing, reminds, us of our manly qualities and our strengths.